BITs & BYTEs Y2K & BEYOND

Timothy V. Kelly

BITs & BYTEs Y2K & BEYOND

Network Technology Services
Pittsburgh, Pennsylvania

Published by:

Network Technology Services
Suite 14E
Chatham Tower
112 Washington Place
Pittsburgh, PENNSYLVANIA 15219
(412)434-5931
http://members.aol.com/ntsy2k/y2k.html

Cover Design: Matthew Kelly

Editor: Thomas Clifton

Library of Congress Catalog Card Number: 98-92207
In-Publication Data:

Kelly, Timothy V.

BITs & BYTEs Y2K & Beyond / Timothy V. Kelly

ISBN 0-9666491-0-9
1. Technology— Sociological Aspects.

98-92207

CIP

Notice of Liability
The information in this book is distributed on an "As is" basis, without warranty. While every precaution has been taken in the preparation of this book, neither author, editor, printer nor Network Technology Services shall have any liability to any person or entity with respect to any liability, loss, or damage caused or alleged to be caused directly or indirectly by the instructions contained in this book or by the computer software and hardware products, as well as the networks and network transports described herein.

Trademarks
Throughout this book trademarked names are used. Rather than put a trademark symbol in every occurrence of a trademarked name, we state that we are using the names only in an editorial fashion and to the benefit of the trademark owner with no intention of infringement of the trademark. Individual trademarks are the property of their respective owners. Product names are mentioned in this book as a matter of information only and do not imply endorsement by the author, editor, printer or publisher. Nor does their mention, infer or imply criticism or disapproval.

Printed on acid-free paper by:

Word Association Publishers
205 5th Avenue
Tarentum, PA 15084
(724) 226-4526

Table of Contents

Acknowledgements

I have been blessed with many opportunities over the past 18. years to have worked in the field of computers and multimedia networks. During this time, our society has evolved from having a great dependence on big, multi-million dollar mainframe computers with limited-if any at all- networking capability, to relatively small, compact desktop, laptop and hand-held computers that cost only a few hundred dollars. Computers today are networkable using one or more of the many methods available for network connectivity. In addition, for 15 of those years, I have had the opportunity to teach as an adjunct faculty member at local universities in the Pittsburgh area. For 10 of the past years I have been fortunate teaching at Duquesne University, one of Pittsburgh's top universities, known principally for its fine schools of law, pharmacy, education, music, arts & sciences and business. I continue to teach courses there mainly in Management Information Systems.

In addition, I am also an adjunct faculty member at two branches of Robert Morris College, a local school offering highly regarded degree programs in both business and communications. There, I teach virtually the same courses as at Duquesne.

This book has been a work in progress since my first days of teaching. I've been riding a roller coaster in search of clarification. Eventually my focus became clear. All digital computer systems and multi-media networks fundamentally must have the information in BITs & BYTEs to process. BITs & BYTEs is where it is at. BITs & BYTEs are the essence of computer and computer network literacy and the essential elements of the Year 2000 (Y2K) set of problems with which North America, Europe, Asia, indeed, all literate nations in the world are now contending. Once I grasped this, free and clear of all the other competing technological elements, I was able to make progress and get this book done. Certainly my many students over the years, in seeking understanding themselves, contributed to this clarification progress.

I'm indebted to Joan Saluga, Dr. Bernard Beranek, Ph.d., and Tom Clifton all of whom admittedly knew neither the BIT or the BYTE, for providing non-technical feedback on syntax, prose and content structure. Lastly, many thanks to Dr. Robert Thompson, Ph.d. who offered specific technical feedback to improve my summary of the Network section.

I would have liked to got more reviews and feedback. However with Y2K fast approaching, we had to get to press! I felt it most important to get the book out now. I would welcome any feedback you the reader may have. Or, if you need directions with any of the concerns you may have regarding The YEAR 2000 (Y2K) set of problems I can be reached at (412) 434-5931. Or via e-mail: tvk2000@aol.com.

Introduction

During the 80's we had the kind of technology which largely required the user to go into the office to get anything done. Technology at that time had very limited capabilities to do home things like word-processing, slow speed remote dial-up to use text-based applications, and, even to some extent play games on the computer with the kids.

Since then the technology has gotten cheaper, faster and presumably better. In addition, equipment has gotten smaller and more efficient. I call it the **SCFB Paradigm**. Smaller, Cheaper, Faster and presumably Better! And this progress shows no signs of slowing down. Individual systems have become accessible anywhere, anytime. The office, the home, the police car-even the delivery truck-have become connected via high-speed networks supporting immediate transfer of "information". In many cases, in a graphical-windows type of presentation format. Point and click have become commonplace.

In effect, the technology has made it possible to support decisions and solve problems more directly than ever before. Little or no wait time is needed to connect the information requestor with the information provider. At the same time, and there seemingly is a down-side to everything, the technology has also made it possible to accelerate chaos and confusion. Consequently, how we manage our information technology becomes paramount.

The impending problems associated with the Year 2000 are a good case in point. Some theorists maintain that the whole Year 2000 (Y2K) set of issues will bring it all to a grinding halt. My intuition tells me that this will not be the case. There will be problems. But none that will be insurmountable. How well we manage our information technology will be the main factor.

The decade of the 1990s has truly been the decade of Telecommunications. The SCFB Paradigm applies also to data, voice and video networks. But more interesting to note, the number of users and organizations getting on the Internet/WEB, as well as the number of virtual private networks (VPNs) being established, is growing more than any other area of computer network technology.

When I consider that 10 years ago Ethernet was a new network standard that ran at 10Mbps (10 Million BITs Per Second) and that today Ethernet technology has surpassed this transmission speed by 100 times, I am completely struck. Today we call it GigaBIT Ethernet.

The GigaBIT is abbreviated Gbps or billion BITs per second. And several other computer network technologies now at the forefront were not yet on the drawing board back in the eighties. Asynchronous Transfer Mode (ATM), not the automated teller machine, is becoming a leading network technology because of its ability to integrate data, voice and video at 155 Mbps over the same cabling system.

In my career, I have endured many definitions of BITs & BYTEs. And as technology changed I observed how these definitions changed as well—usually becoming more confusing and non-specific. Now that we can process chaos from any location at nearly the speed of light, it has become a critical socio-technological factor for the corporate user, consumer, technocrat, and any student of the computer or computer network, to truly comprehend what exactly we are dealing with when we process BITs & BYTEs. Subsequent chapters are an attempt to clarify these most important concepts.

The ensuing chapters are offered to you herein with a label warning. This is not a one-read book. Also it is not a book for the computer scientist or the computer engineer. It is a book for those who want, and need to truly know, the BIT and the BYTE.

In other words, if you really want to know the BIT and the BYTE, you will probably need to go through the book more than once,-maybe a few times. Although the media tends to oversimplify BIT and BYTE related stories, the fact of the matter is, BITs and BYTEs are somewhat complex. But then so is your checkbook. So is driving a car, filing your income tax, or worse, having your accountant file your taxes on your behalf, because with this option you still need to comprehend your return. And in addition to that, you get billed for it! Reading the calorie chart on the box of a frozen dinner is complicated, but you get through it.

And I believe we need to get through BITs & BYTEs, because Y2K is upon us. Y2K is going to happen whether we understand BITs & BYTEs or not. And let us not suffer any delusions here. Y2K will not be a pretty picture. I'm not proclaiming doomsday, but there will be problems across the board, the nation, and the world.

Dedication

To Matt, Christal, Gabe and Laural
for whom the turning of the new millennium will provide
greater opportunities founded upon late technology,
requiring new standards for living.

PART 1: The BIT

1

Why Do I Need to Know the BIT?

My interest in the computer began in the early sixties. It was a movie called "Babes In Toyland" that spawned my fascination. The young professor in the movie had developed a colorful machine contraption which had lots of different kinds of connections and flashing lights. He called it "automation". In my favorite scene, he made a toy by keying in some toy feature requirements and throwing the switch. After a few seconds of strange noises and flashing lights out came a toy soldier. I was left with utter amazement.

Although young at the time, I was 'taken hostage' by the lights in the "Babes" movie. It didn't make sense to me. I couldn't let go of this scene. From that point on, I became captivated by computer technology. Anytime a movie would have a scene where some type of computer was employed with the lights, I would wonder how it was possible.

How could this happen? Knowing it to be only a movie, in later years as I reflected on this, what intrigued me most was how the producers could expect the audience to begin to believe. And in later time, as the media continued to lament the growing and evolving power of the computer, I continued to remember the scene from

"Babes". I continue to this day to wonder about those flashing lights.

I'm in awe when I see how much computer technology has changed. And although computer technology continues to evolve rapidly, the basic operating principles of the digital computer are still in place. We have just developed thousands of different and more effective ways to put these principals into practice.

Any way you shake it with computer technology, what it comes down to essentially is BITs & BYTEs. To know BITs & BYTEs is to truly know the computer and the computer network. The flashing lights in the 'Babes' movie were an exaggerated attempt to illustrate the processing of BITs & BYTEs through a make-believe computer. There was a feeble attempt back then to explain the 'magical power' of the computer, and much was left unsaid.

Over the years, many attempts have been made to explain BITs & BYTEs. However other "worthy news" elements of the improving computer and computer-related technology have been stealing the show for the most part since the computer's inception. During the sixties, mainframes with their storage disks and diskettes were the big deal. In the seventies, minicomputers and the growth of computer networks stole the show. In the eighties there was a convergence of newsworthy elements like the personal computer (PC), Local Area Networks (LAN), the evolution of the chip from the Intel 8088 to what today is known as the Pentium II chip. And many many more changes and improvements. Most of these technologies would illustrate and attempt to define aspects of BITs & BYTEs. But at best these were incomplete attempts. None of the media-promoted definitions of BITs & BYTEs would ever really take hold.

The media continually glosses over the BITs & BYTEs essentials in favor of the application uses of the latest computer development. Broad-minded, dedicated and overworked executives, as well as parents and teachers are continually portrayed as people who for many reasons cannot take the time to focus on understanding BITs & BYTEs, because this type of information is usually presented in a tedious and technical manner.

A clear, comprehensive definition of BITs & BYTEs has not yet been promulgated. But the need to understand the essential elements of computers and computer networks is needed now as never before, because the technology is changing so rapidly.

Part I of this book is all about the BIT. We will go over the inception of the BIT on what is considered the very first computer, namely the ENIAC. If you can understand the inception of the BIT on the ENIAC, which used vacuum tube technology, you can conquer the entire Computer Glossary of terms. The BIT is the most essential element of the computer and the computer network. Knowing the BIT means you can become a leader of computer related technical knowledge in your company, in your classroom, or in your family.

Knowing the BIT will enable you to have a better comprehension of computers and computer networks. This applies irrespective of what model computer or what type of computer network, because the BIT is the foundation upon which all computer-related technologies are built. Even the latest and greatest computer, however well today it does its thing, still must translate its information down to the BIT level to process. This is why the title of this book has the wording, "Y2K and Beyond" because no matter how much faster, cheaper or smaller the technology gets in the new millennium, it will still need to translate down to the BIT-level to process. There may be numerous new ways to network BITs, but the machine-level processes on the individual computer still must move BIT-encoded electricity to compute, store and display results.

Although leading the charge in gaining computer knowledge is reason enough, there are many other reasons why you need to know the BIT. For executives responsible for purchasing computers in the company, you will need to review, support or reject budgetary line items for increased costs related to the company's computer or computer network. For example, your MIS Manager or MIS Team is requesting additional funds for the coming year to replace N number of computers with the current day computers. If you know the BIT, you can ask the right questions. For example, "why do we need new computers?". The MIS manager may explain that the company needs 32-BIT processors capable of running the company's software more efficiently. Or the manager may say we need PCs with a 64-BIT Data BUS to handle all of the concurrent applications employees will be running. (Concurrent means to keep multiple applications running or "active" on the computer at the same time.) Concurrent operations are becoming commonplace in the business world. Knowing the BIT enables you to readily understand key factors through which to differentiate computers based on power and speed. Differences between a 32-BIT and 64-BIT processor, or 32-BIT and 64-BIT Data BUS become tangible in terms of their actual power.

Similarly teachers and parents are asked numerous BIT-related questions from curious and inquisitive young minds. The BIT relates directly to the speed and power of the computer and the computer network. Most young people are fascinated with these characteristics about computers in general. A student may want to know how big of a file he or she can download from the WEB. Or how long it will take to download a file of a particular size. (Download means to copy down or transfer, a file of BYTEs from a file-server which is located somewhere on the network to the hard disk or diskette located on your particular computer.) Knowing the BIT enables you to respond to such questions in a supportive yet accurate manner.

Knowing the BIT will also enhance your understanding of the BYTE and hence files which are made up of BYTEs. Understanding the BIT is relative to all other computer and computer network related subjects, including comprehension of the BYTE. Thats right. You need to know the BIT in order to know the BYTE. Remember this book is about BITs...and BYTEs.

The BYTE is what the 'Year 2000' problem is all about. Many issues abound at the current time concerning what will happen to our automated society when the calendar reaches January 1, 2000. Computers have keyed on the last two digits of the calendar year since their inception over fifty years ago. How will the computer now deal with processing a year, which ends in 00? This is the 64 million-dollar question. And this is a BYTE problem. As such it is also a BIT problem too, because BYTEs are made up of BITs. I will discuss the BYTE in Part II of this book.

In addition to the BIT, knowing the BYTE is an integral part of knowing the computer and computer network technology. The BYTE is the foundation for several other important elements, much the same way that the BIT is the foundation for many important elements, such as the language of computers, power as expressed through BUS size, and the speed of computer networks expressed in 'BITs-per-second' or 'bps'.

Moreover, and I will talk about this subject in greater detail later in the book, computer networks have grown enormously since they became standardized in the 1980s. Small networks now must connect to larger networks, which must connect to still larger networks. Each network connection, from the smallest of networks to those that are global, uses 'bandwidth' as a key design and costing factor. Bandwidth is measured in BITs-per-second transmission rates. If you know the BIT you know what it means to transmit N number of BITs-per-second. And you will readily discern what the dollar costs are for that bandwith.

The Internet and World Wide WEB are good examples of external networks that can be connected into via corporate and school networks or from your computer at home. Most companies have their own proprietary networks, which are being linked to the Internet. Connection to the Internet and World Wide WEB has become a major requirement in order to do business in today's global marketplace. Similarly schools are moving fast to get on the World Wide WEB via the Internet. And newer, faster technologies for connecting the home to the Internet are begining to hit the marketplace.

Bandwidth of such networks is a managerial characteristic of the network that needs to be monitored regularly, because a large part of the cost of operating a network or an individual network connection is in the recurring charges (i.e. hourly, daily, monthly). The charges are predicated upon how much bandwidth is being consumed over specified periods of time. The more users there are on the network, the more business being processed, the more bandwidth is required.

Many questions relevant to a BIT perspective on computers and computer networks abound. Do the computer network lines need to operate at 56Kbps (or 56,000 bps). Does the computer network require 1.536Mbps (that is 1,536,000 bps)? Costs between just these 2 bandwidth options vary greatly. And there are numerous other bandwidth and throughput options to consider. (Bandwidth is the amount of BITs that can possibly be transferred over the line in any given second. Throughput, also measured in bps, is what actually gets transferred over the line.)

You can have, and all medium-to-large-size companies do have multiple sites, which generate combinations of bandwidth- related charges. Some sites may have low-bandwidth needs, and other sites may have high bandwidth needs. But all site's bandwidth would be measured in BITs, and the cost would be based on BIT-per-second bandwidth transmission rates at each respective site.

Have you ever been asked a computer BIT-related question? I've been teaching computers at the college level and community level since 1983. I would need a computer to count how many times I've been asked such questions. A few follow here:

From a woman in her fifties: "The book says a BIT is an "ON" or an "OFF" electrical state. Do you have to turn it "OFF" to make it work?

From a sixth grader: "My DAD says electricity is to a computer what gasoline is to a car. Where is the computer ignition key? I can't find it anywhere.

From a Freshman in College: "Do the computers in the lab support 32-BIT processing?

From a Junior in High School: "Its says that the computer comes with an integrated 56K modem. Will this work if I want to 'surf the WEB'?".

And there are many other related questions I could list. All of them do not directly express a need to know the BIT, but all of them require a response founded in true comprehension of the BIT.

The point is, that in the classroom you can expect, and should receive many questions, particularly if it is a 'first' course related to the computer. Even in a non-computer-related course, the computer will impose itself in many ways, what with the media and the expanding use of the Internet and WEB in all course-subject domains.

For parents, the challenge is formidable, because in addition to dealing with the growing individuality of their children, they are frequently confronted with educational systems, that are still behind the pace at which computer technology is evolving. Their hope is that they will be able to find schools and teachers who are able to deliver up-to-date information. To find those leaders who keep pace with the industry.

And kids, not faced with the confusion we adults have had to deal with, acquire computer knowledge much faster than older people. This is true, at least generally, with the 'procedural' things which are required to operate the computer. My children amazed me at the speed with which they were able to get on the computer and operate it with no prior training. When Matt & Christal were 7 and 5 respectively, they were using the keyboard and doing word-processing and of course games. Gabe & Laural, at 3 and 1, enjoyed playing games. In particular, games that emphasized keyboard skills.

Nowadays, there is great concern about restricting or censoring child-access to portions of the Internet and WEB. Many parents do not know what the WEB is, let alone know how to advise their growing children on how they should access various WEB Sites. The BIT is the first essential element for folks to comprehend. Parents need to know BIT because it is at the BIT level that everything is controlled on the computer and the computer network. WEB addresses like WWW.whatever.com, are actually BIT-encoded numeric addresses. Your computer and the various pieces of hardware on the network, in establishing and maintaining your network connection, translate this address at the BIT level.

Knowledge of the BIT will help parents understand the quality or speed of any computer connection, including connections to the Internet and World Wide WEB. Knowing the BIT enables parents also to truly comprehend the volumes of information, which can be processed in any particular computer application. Gaining access is one thing. Maintaining accessibility is another. However, knowing the BIT is the foundation for both of these because you will have that 'machine' level of understanding about computer and computer network characteristics. This will limit your frustration when things are not working right. You will understand that it is not magic, but technology based on the evolution and adaptation of many technologies that have come before. Everything from light bulbs to radio and television are technologies which relate directly to the evolution of computers and their networks.

For executives, parents, teachers and many others who may be responsible for users of the computer or computer network, knowing the BIT will provide you with that necessary keystone for building computer knowledge in others. It will help you in your company, your classroom and in working with and guiding the growing interest in the computer. Knowing the BIT is the foundation upon which to build true comprehension of the computer and the computer network.

2

The BIT Definitions

In the late fifties, the media began to make the public aware of the nuances and technological breakthroughs involving computer technology. Every day, the press, the broadcast news, and various other media presented the latest evolution in the continuing saga of the computer. Larger, more expensive and faster variations on the computer and computer-related devices would be illustrated in some form in the media. In those days "Big" was the preeminent characteristic of whether or not you or your company had the best available computer technology. The answer to the question "What kind of computer should we get?"...in those days was "Get a BIG computer!". The more space it took to install and operate, the more likely was the perception that it was better. BITs & BYTEs were not even a consideration, because there was only one kind of computer-'BIG'. And there were not yet any computer networks. The 'BIG' perception, which because of the position of computer technology at the time, was fitting. This new office equipment now being used to process office data had to be bigger to accommodate all of the hardware components needed to enable it to operate.

Computer manufacturers became vested in this "BIG" view of the computer. Their assembly lines, marketing initiatives, and customer support services all followed a paradigm of the computer system being "BIG". Consequently IBM and those companies which sought to operate in the "BIG" computer market necessarily had to set up large organizations with enormous overhead to compete in the marketplace. As a result, computer technology during those times became expensive, relatively speaking. And the expense of the computer then had not yet been correlated with the metrics associated today with BITs & BYTEs. For instance, the more BITs you can process over a given period of time, 'the bigger the bang for your computer buck', was not yet a factor in purchasing a computer.

But when the "BIG" paradigm began to shift in the seventies with the inception into the computer marketplace of the mini-computer, a divergent set of computer-technology related developments began to occur. "BIG" was questioned. "Does it really have to be so big? Could it be smaller? " Yes, it could, depending on the job the computer would be used for and how those applications would be processed.

Early insights into computer usage offered ways to process similar amounts of information using less computer processing capacity, or fewer numbers of BITs & BYTEs. This meant that computers did not have to be so big. Smaller computers meantless expensive computers. This in turn meant greater deployment of computer technology across the marketplace. Small and medium-sized companies could now afford the less costly, although still not cheap, computers.

Fueled by the momentum of the seventies, a technological revolution of computer technology developed in the eighties and nineties and continues to evolve to this day. Personal computers or PCs for the desktop were introduced in the early 1980s. Smaller computers could now process more BITs & BYTEs than the previous generation of larger, more expensive computers. Laptop, Notebook and 'Palm Top' computers came onto the scene in the 1990s. The decreasing cost and size of computers made more computers available to yet a larger part of the population. This further reduced the cost and fueled even more the continuing growth and transformation of the computer in its size, cost and function.

Whereas the fifties and sixties brought about a "BIG" paradigm, which continuously evolved to a "SMALL" paradigm, the new technological process has become: "Smaller, Cheaper, Faster and Better". Today, computers are the smallest in terms of physical size then ever before. Computers, BIT for BYTE, have never been cheaper. And computers today have never been faster. All of this presumably means the average Joe or Jane on the street, whether it be Wall Street or Maple Street, gets a much better value for their computer buck.

Defining the BIT

BITs & BYTEs are still the essential elements of computers & computer networks. Although smaller, cheaper, faster and presumably better; the computer, in whatever form it takes, still processes in BITs & BYTEs. These are the two single-most important elements of understanding computers and computer networks. This book is about BITs & BYTEs, and about relating BITs & BYTEs to the computer and computer network technology. Know Ye the BIT and the BYTE, my friend and you will know in its most intimate terms the computer & the computer network—the most important technologies of the current century and of the new millennium—which in a couple of years is about to engulf all of society.

If you were to take all of the computer dictionaries available today and boil down all of the prevailing definitions on BITs you would end up, for the most part, with the table of definitions following here.

Prevailing Definitions of a BIT

1. A 'contraction of the the two words 'Binary and digIT'.

2. A one, that is number '1' or a zero, that is number '0'. And yes! '0' is a number.

3. The smallest 'UNIT' of information on a computer.

4. An 'ON' or an 'OFF' state.

5. A 'HIGH or a 'LOW' pulse.

Lets take #1. A concern with grammatical correctness is immediately obvious. Since when can we contract two seemingly unrelated terms-one an adjective, the other a noun, such as 'Binary' and 'DigIT' respectively? The fact is that it is not correct grammar. Yet the BIT as we now call it across the world of computers and computer networks, is one of two single most important elements in the understanding of how computers work, and how we utilize and pay for networkin computers. This definition has crept into our culture over the past 50 years, and today is indeed promulgated quite extensively.

Definition #2. It is perhaps simple to see that these are nothing more than 2 digits. If you know mathematics you may know that these are the two numbers which make up the entire set of numbers in the

Base 2 numbering system. Just these two numbers! You may be wondering what meaning there could be in what seemingly are two unconnected digits. And a fact about this particular definition is that unless you have prior knowledge in computer engineering or computer science, it will be difficult to make a connection with much of anything having to do with the computer. The reality of this definition is that it merely represents what the BIT actually is. Representing something is vastly different from being that which is represented. Philosophical I grant you, but as you will see-accurate.

Definition #3 "can" be accurate depending upon what perspective you bring to it. If you view the "BIT" from the "machine level" there are many instances in which a single "BIT" is "informational", largely to the computer engineering and computer scientist domains. However, at the "highest level", the level where we humans use our natural languages to communicate, the "BIT" is far far far from being "Information". Still, this is the definition you are most likely to hear from the computer sales person.

Definitions #4 and #5 are the most accurate of the predominant definitions. These two accurately depict two valid, different and unique flavors of the BIT and what the BIT is, actually and factually. The shortcoming here is that we are back to the domain of the computer engineers and the computer scientists.

At this point, I want to begin to clarify the BIT confusion. It is here that I intend to finalize and summarize the BIT definition. In the subsequent chapters of Part I, I will explain and clarify the BIT from its inception to its most current meanings.

Given that the BIT definition, from its very inception, has started off with a grammatical error, you can imagine what numbers and varieties of computer terminology have evolved since the inception of the BIT. I could do a complete volume of books on the BIT etymology alone.

Therefore, in defining the BIT, I'm limiting my material here to: explaining how the BIT got started, how it emerged as the core metric ingredient of internal computer operations, and how it became the single most important factor used by computer network provider companies in pricing out the use of computer networks for their customers, both corporate and consumer alike.

Along with the above summary definitions as shown in the preceding table, I offer you my definition of a BIT:

It is a binary unit which is either an 'ON' or 'OFF' state, or a corresponding 'HIGH' or 'LOW' pulse, of electricity, light, electro-magnetic or electro-optical matter. A BIT is the smallest, single, metrical unit of active memory, permanent storage and/or processing on digital computers and networks. BIT metrics are used extensively in costing out computers, telecommunication networks. In addition, they are used to evaluate the speed and power of same. Factors such as BUS and processor size are measured by the number of single BITs which can be processed in any single moment in time. Network bandwidth and throughput are measured in BITs-per-second (bps). Machine-level engineers use the binary mathematical language of ones (1s) and zeroes (0s) in the programs they create to represent the 'ON' and 'OFF' states, or the 'HIGH' and 'LOW' pulses which are then generated by executing their programs in support of innumerable applications. The BIT has emerged as the single most important factor in determining the speed of computers, multimedia networks (i.e. data, voice, video), and related technology.

Failure to know the BIT is not an option! You must know it!

What Makes Knowing the BIT An Important Priority

With a good understanding of the BIT, you will be prepared to take on anything related to computer or computer networks. Students of the computer and computer network will be able to see the broader aspects of this important technology. Like we all need to breath air, eat food and sleep, computers and computer networks operate at the most fundamental level (i.e. machine level) on BITs. You will be able to more effectively manage company computer resources and guide others in an optimal way when they inquire about the many BIT related computer and computer network topics. Also, you will be able to see the computer big picture in which learning this important technology becomes a progressive journey along which you will become computer literate. Essentially, computers and computer networks will become not only easy for you to use but entirely possible for you to understand.

Knowing the BIT is to the computer or the computer network what DNA is to the human being. We are not going to get nearly as technical as we would with covering DNA. But it is true that DNA provides the genetic coding for all of the systems in the human being, including such things as circulation, neurology, vision, etc.

Similarly, the BIT is the core element of Machine language, which is the fundamental coding language of all computers and computer networks. Machine language is also known as binary language. All things on the computer, no matter what hardware or what software is being used, must ultimately translate into machine language in order to be processed. Machine language or binary language is all BITs, nothing but BITs.

The computer is inherently a binary machine. That is, no matter what the computer processes, it must ultimately be translated or converted into "Binary Form". This is perhaps the most important point to comprehend about the computer and the computer network. The "Binary Form" means that the electricity flowing through the computer's circuitry is "Coded" using the binary numbering system known in mathematics as Base 2.

The "Coding" into binary form, although done manually by the early computer scientists, has itself been automated over the years. This is possible because of the inherent "Binary Nature" of electricity. Electricity is either "ON" or "OFF" And therefore has only 2 possible states. Likewise the Base 2 numbering system has only 2 digits, "1" and "0". It is a simple matter to represent the 2 states of electricity with the Base 2 numbering system.

Modern computer and computer network technology has advanced to a point where many other new techniques are being used to translate and transfer BITs of information other than those which use strictly the ON and OFF electrical states. They are the HIGH and LOW light pulse codes over fiber-optic cable systems, radio signals using High and Low modulation to support cellular connections, satellite, microwave signaling, and others. However, whatever techniques or technology is (are) deployed to support the transfer, the encoded signals must ultimately translate down to BITs. That is, Base 2, Binary, on the computer in order to process. The same way it was done, albeit much slower then, on the first and early computers. And it is the same binary encoding on all computers developed since then, including the networks to which these computers connect.

There is an important distinction between how the computer processes purely mathematical information and how it translates textual information. Mathematical data has to be processed using the Binary, Base 2 numbering system, which is inherent to the electrical or ON/OFF state nature of electricity. It can be said that these calculations are completed by the movement of the relevant BITs into and out of the microchips known as Registers located on the part of the computer known as the Arithmetic Logic Unit or ALU for short.

The ALU Registers are located on the motherboard. They have circuit traces which connect them to other parts of the motherboard, such as the CPU and Memory. The ALU receives in and transmits out results, which are used in mathematical calculations. Calculation results in BIT-form are moved into Main Memory for display, to be printed out and or to be saved in permanent storage.

Conversely, for the nonmathematical data, like plain text, the user's keystrokes go in and get converted immediately by whatever standardized character encoding set is installed on the computer. Today PCs or individual computers come mostly with ASCII (American Standard Code for Information Interchange) or more recently with UNICODE (Uniform International Character Encoding). UNICODE actually incorporates the entire ASCII set of character codes in its more voluminous set of codes. Actually UNICODE converts keystrokes for every character in every known language of the world. ASCII merely includes our well-known alphabet, plus some other special characters and numbers.

Anyway, the pre-installed character encoding set converts the user's keystrokes to the necessary coded ON & OFF states to represent textual things like letters, numbers, special and graphical characters. In the case of UNICODE, for example, the keystroke would be converted to 16 BITs, because UNICODE is a 16-BIT encoding set. Whereas ASCII and EBCDIC (Extended Binary Coded Decimal Interchange Coded) for comparison are 7- and 8-BIT codes respectively. EBCDIC is used on IBM mainframes. The type of preinstalled character encoding set is an indicator of the computer's versatility and power.

Another important measure of the power of any computer would be the size of the computer's main Data BUS. I point it out here because the Data BUS is a component that is measured in BITs. Sometimes the Data BUS is referred to as having a certain "BIT width". For instance, 32-BIT width or 64-BIT width. This refers specifically to how many BITs can be put on the Data BUS at any given moment in time. The Data BUS is to the computer what the main artery is to a highway system. Currently a 64-BIT Data BUS is considered to be the most powerful in the individual or PC line of computers. Projections for the future on how the size of the Data BUS will change extend all the way up to a 1024-BIT width on the computer utilizing a purely laser-optic method of signal processing versus what we now know to be purely electrical.

Knowing the BIT means to know the future of computers and computer networks. The speed and size of this technology is founded upon the BIT. The BIT is the single-most important element of the computer and computer network.

The BIT and Numbering Systems

Most folks in our American society are familiar with the Base 10 numbering system. They may not realize they are familiar with "Base

10", but we use it every day, perhaps without thinking about it, because we know it so well. Base 10 is the numbering system on which our U.S. currency is based. In "Base 10" we have 10 digits. For instance, 10 pennies equal a dime, 10 dimes equal a dollar, 10 one hundred dollars equal one thousand dollars and so on.

Each number expressed in Base 10 represents a specific position. For example, the number 1,258 has 4 positions. These positions are 1s, 10s, 100s and 1000s. Therefore the number 1,258 has 8 in the 1s position, 5 in the 10s position, 2 in the 100s position and 1 in the 1000s position. The number is expressed as "one-thousand two-hundred fifty-eight".

Think of it in terms of U.S. currency. Everyone knows money. Even all the other banks and countries of the world use a Base 10 numbering system. Have you ever had to exchange U.S. dollars for pesos, marks or yen? There is a conversion table preset based on the current value of our dollar compared to each one of these foreign currencies. One dollar, for instance, may equal 4.5 Yen. The baseline conversion, or multiple, like in this example: 4.5 to 1 is predetermined by the banking authorities. And it changes, based on the economics of the day.

In a similar way, the computer needs to convert Base 10 numbers to Base 2 numbers, and after processing, Base 2 numbers back to Base 10 numbers. The major difference between the currency example and the computer is....that the computer never changes its baseline conversion or multiple. The computer is always and forever....binary, that means the baseline will always be Base 2.

In Base 10 we have 10 unique, possible digits that are used to express any number. These digits are 0,1,2,3,4,5,6,7,8 and 9. And it is by using some combination of these 10 digits, across the applicable Base 10 positions as discussed above, that we can express any number in Base 10. For example, to express the number 9,478,983; I place a 9 in the 'millions position', a 4 in the hundred-thousands position, and so forth. Each digit placed is unique to its position, even though the same digit can be used over again at different positions.

Many mathematical theorists over the years experimented with different ways to "expedite" mathematical calculations. The Abacus was one practical implementation of Base 10 theory. They used to teach the Abacus in the early elementary school years here in America. (This was before wide-spread deployment of desktop and other computers in the school systems.)

The challenge here though becomes one of relating the conversion of Base 10 numbers to Base 2, which is the binary numbering system. Because everything in the computer comes down to being translated into binary.

And this is where the early inventors discovered that vacuum tubes could be used to implement directly the binary numbering system in a fully-electric manner. The vacuum tubes could be made to hold an electric charge signifying an "ON" state or the binary equivalent of a one (1). And when the tube was not charged or had a reduced charge, it was in the "OFF" state or the binary equivalent of a zero (0). The '1' and '0' merely represented the reality of an "ON" state or an "OFF" state respectively with the vacuum tube.

Once invented, the computer was used strictly for calculating in Binary or Base 2. And when the processing of a calculation was complete the result in Base 2 would have to be converted into Base 10 so that it could be readily understood. The process of converting the Base 2 results was done manually at first. It was already overly complicated to make the early computer work in binary with 18,000 vacuum tubes. Can you imagine what it would take in vacuum tubes to represent the Base 10 numbering system?

Base 2 is actually much less complicated than our very own Base 10. This is because in Base 2 or Binary, as we say, there are only 2 digits. Two,... that's it. And these two digits are the one (1) and the zero (0). Like Base 10 which has a total of 10 digits including 0, and can repeat any of the ten digits to express any number, Base 2 numbers can repeat either of its two digits as many times as necessary to express any number.

And it is by using some combination of zeroes and ones that we can develop coding systems in Base 2. In order to express a result in Base 10 which we all know and understand, binary or Base 2 calculations must be converted to Base 10. The process of converting to Base 10 had to be done manually on the first computers, but this process is completely automated on modern day computers.

So the 'ON' and 'OFF' nature of electricity as illustrated through the vacuum tube on the very first computer was highly conducive to the application of the Binary Numbering System or Base 2. The '1' was associated with the "ON" state of the vacuum tube and the '0' was associated with the vacuum tube's off state. Electricity is inherently binary. Therefore the Base 2 numbering system could be applied directly to the fully electric digital computer. In summary then, two states "ON" or "OFF". Two digits '1' and '0'. Electricity is either ON or OFF. As a result, we can code electricity with '1' and '0'.

The theory behind numbering systems being applied to fully electrical digital computers was completed long before 1943. Binary was considered to be the front-runner of any of the other numbering systems because it is based on two digits, a zero and a one. And electricity as understood at the time has only 2 possible states—"ON" or

"OFF". The application of the binary numbering system to the theory occurred many times over and had been proven on paper more than once. The challenge of the time however was in harnessing the electricity to make it work.

Today we no longer use vacuum tubes. However the challenge continues today with the 'SCFB Paradigm'. Conquering electricity using Smaller, Cheaper, Faster & Better techniques is the consummate passion of companies that make computers and computer networks. Computers and computer network technology have advanced tremendously beyond the replacement of the vacuum tubes. Modern day computers employ semiconductors and integrated circuitry to optimize the 'binary state' of things. But the computer's magical power still remains the same in its most fundamental requirement of needing to process information in the binary form. Binary means Base 2 numbering system. The computer and the computer network are inherently binary. This binary baseline will not change even in light of today's continuing and evolving computer related technologies.

The good news is that the need to convert binary results into Base 10 has been completely automated. Specialized programmers skilled in mathematics are no longer needed to do complex manual calculations for each and every application on the computer. Operational and procedural savvy combined with BITs & BYTEs literacy is all it takes to master the modern day computer. Now if you want to get into engineering and programming of the computer and computer network at the machine level...go for it! Like many fields we need people in these professions.

My focus in the above has been on the mathematical. You might ask 'What about the nonmathematical?' Fair question. The answer is that the computer does the nonmathematical using standardized coding systems that are hardwired into the computer by the manufacturer. These standard codes convert letters, special characters and nonmathematical numbers to a predefined set of 'ON' and 'OFF' states. In the EBCDIC code, the letter 'A' for example has a code equal to some combination of 8 ones and zeroes. In reality, inside the computer these 8 ones and/or zeroes, represent the corresponding 'ON' and 'OFF' states which would, during processing, pulsate through the computer. The people that manufacture the computers, represent this predefined set using 1s and 0s, back at the shop when they engineer the computer's standard character set into the circuitry and hardware of the processor box.

For those of us that use the computer these days we rarely, if at all, will need to delve into this level of code. But it is useful to know that one of a handful of different standard character sets is loaded on your computer at the factory. Analysts expect the 16-BIT UNICODE to become dominant.

Sometimes these character codes are referred to as being "higher level". This means that they are not purely binary. They are precoded in binary and then get translated into machine language. This differs from a pure mathematical number which translates directly into machine language. For example, to add 2 numbers, the computer would take the binary, or Base 2 form of the first number, and add it to the binary or Base 2 form of the other number and store the result in binary or Base 2. It would do this for any set of numbers to be added. There is no pre-coded standard. It is purely binary or Base 2.

A letter such as 'A' would first be converted to its predefined set of ones and zeroes before being processed. Viewed in this manner, character processing on a computer is largely predictable and fixed because the number of BITs involved is predefined. With the mathematical there is a higher degree of variability based on the size of the numbers involved in the calculations. The size of the numbers involved will determine how many BITs are needed to process and calculate.

Perhaps the most touted character coding system currently is UNICODE, which predefines characters based on 16 BITs. UNICODE is capable of translating the character sets for every language known to man. UNICODE also incorporates the EBCDIC and ASCII character coding sets, which have been the two mainstays of character processing over the past 30 years.

Imagine doing an e-mail to your Mother who speaks and reads very little English. But let's say she is fluent in Polish. After keying in the e-mail message, you highlight the text with your mouse. You then click on the language translator button. And then click on Polish. The screen now shows your e-mail message completely in Polish. This is the type of thing that a computer with UNICODE hardwired in can do for you.

And lastly, once again, no matter what coding system is being used, mathematical or nonmathematical, whatever is being processed on the computer or the computer network must ultimately be translated down to machine language. Machine language is binary and we use ones and zeroes to represent respectively "ON" and "OFF" states. In the case of computer networking the "HIGH" and "LOW" pulses are represented respectively by ones and zeroes.

What you, the user will see however, on the screen, will be the characters or numbers. The 'On' and 'OFF' or 'HIGH' and 'LOW' nature of computer and computer network processing is completely transparent. And it all happens at nearly the speed of light.

The BIT in Mathematical, Textual and Other Terms

With vacuum tube technology reflecting back, it is rather simplistic to see, with this obsolete technology, how an "ON" or "OFF" BIT was generated. But let's remember that the computer back then was used strictly for calculating mathematical problems. Today the computer does much more than strictly that. And the computer has advanced to a stage where the old vacuum tubes have been replaced by ultra-high-performance integrated circuitry.

As such, today we have a few other ways in which to "Binarilize" BITs (i.e. code as 1 and 0) to support transmission and transfer within the computer and over the computer network. Computer and computer network related electricity, fiber-optic signals even radio signals among other techniques use "High" and "Low" pulse codes to represent BITs. HIGH pulse like a BIT 1 corresponds to an "ON" state, and LOW pulse like BIT 0 equals an "OFF" state. Whatever the technique used to support BIT transfers, whether inside the computer itself or over computer networks it still comes down to the binary or Base 2, as we have been discussing.

I call this level, where everything is binary or Base 2, the "Machine Level". Everything here is moving in "ON" and "OFF" states or "HIGH" and "LOW" pulses. The 'machine level' is the level where the electricity is processing BITs—not translating other coded forms (higher levels) of what eventually becomes binary. Although there is a major distinction between the way the computer treats the mathematical and the way the computer processes other applications which are "text-based", it all comes down to the machine level to be processed. This includes applications like word-processing, spreadsheeting, e-mail, etc. What you see on the screen actually exists at the time you see it on the screen in memory. When you save, print or transfer data on the computer or over the network, these functions are said to be completed at the machine level.

Many added techniques, and new hardware over the years have augmented and improved the computer's capabilities with the mathematical. For example Reduced Instruction Set Computers or RISC computers are designed to process the mathematical more efficiently. Also mathematical "co-processors" have been added to some computers to step up their capability for processing calculations. And today's MMX technology has truly expanded and sharpened the speed of computer processing. MMX is a new technique standing for **M**atrix **M**athematical e**X**tensions that speeds up computer processing.

But regardless of which techniques are employed, the computer ultimately must have the numbers involved in the calculation in binary form in order to process. This is the nature of the computer beast. It is always and forever binary! Binary....binary....binary! And binary means Base 2, which means mathematics using 1s and 0s. Today, as it was on the very first computer 50 years ago, it is a binary world. And the computer will remain binary beyond the year 2000. Binary, Base 2 is the computer's only true language. Remember this and you can say that you comprehend half the battle of truly knowing the computer.

This is the heart of why binary works so well with electricity. The computer does not really know we humans are representing its "ON" and "OFF" states with a lot of 1s and 0s. The computer, like any other electrical device, processes its electrical current. It does its electrical thing blindly. This is why many experts refer to the computer as a "DUMB MACHINE". The computer itself does not have the brains to calculate on its own. It processes electrical current which is encoded in binary by us humans.

The challenge, if there is one here, is to understand that the phenomenon of electricity supports inherently the binary nature of digital computer processing. Electricity is either ON or OFF. Therefore we can directly apply binary coding to calculate in pure Electricity. Network connections are founded upon the technology of being able to translate binary coded signals, such as those in "ON"or "OFF"states, into conversely "HIGH" or "LOW" pulses. And then convert them back at the other end of the network connection.

The processing of textual information on the computer builds on the inherent binary nature of the digital computer. Essentially, in order to process textual information made up largely of the alphabetic, a technique for getting character-based information coded in binary, became the preeminent challenge for the early computer scientists.

The mechanism developed to meet this challenge was to assign a binary code (you could say a binary "pre-code") to every character to be processed. That meant every upper-case letter, lower-case letter, and special characters as well. Because the computer must have it in binary form to process, every character had to have a unique binary pre-code. An upper-case 'A' had to have a different code then a lower-case 'a' because the computer had no other way to make the distinction. To the computer an upper-case 'A' is completely different from a lower-case 'a'. So the binary coding system developed for this purpose had to accommodate all of the upper and lower case letters as well as the special characters like parentheses, commas, periods, etc.

On the surface, the challenge of developing a binary coding system for characters of the alphabet does not seem like it would be that complicated. But back in the early days when it took one vacuum tube to set a single BIT, the burning question was "What is it going to take to code the letters of the alphabet?"

As is the case with most technological progressions, developers look at what has evolved, prior to pioneering something new. It just so happens that there was some precedent for the binary encoding of character-based information. A system known as the Baudot code had been developed by a Frenchman of that same name in the 1930s. The Baudot Code used a total of five elements to encode each letter of the alphabet in upper-case. There were also a few special characters used in Baudot for a total of 32 directly encoded characters. The Code also had a dual key combination for changing case, like the 'Shift' key. When this key was used in combination with the respective letter's key it would do a case shift. Given this, we could say that the Baudot Code actually had a total of 64 code combinations.

The Baudot Code was used mainly in the transmission of telegraph messages. The elements used were simply dots and dashes. How is that for a binary code? Remember earlier we said that the binary, Base 2 system used just two digits, the '1' and '0'. And we said that the electricity which the computer ran on was inherently binary, because electricity is either on or off. So it became a no-brainer to build on the binary concept of the Baudot code in order to support the textual characters needed on the early computers.

Compared to modern day computers, the Baudot system was very limited. But the concept used in the Baudot code for the telegraph was used to build onto for a character-based, binary coding system. They just simply made the dashes represent the 1s and dots to represent the 0s. Voila! Instant binary code for the computer to process the non-mathematical. But Baudot only covered 32 or 64 characters, depending on how you view it. Each character had 5 positions, that is 2 to the 5 power for a total of 32 codes. Therefore it had to be extended to at least permit all of the characters of the alphabet, both upper-case and lower-case. Using the Baudot concept and a little redesign, a new code was developed.

The result initially was a system called Binary Coded Decimal or BCD for short, which used 6 positions to encode the letters of the alphabet. That is, each letter and special character had a unique set or combination of zeroes and ones that totaled 6 BITs.

By using 6 BITs per character the early developers hoped to resolve the limitations inherent with the 5-BIT Baudot code. BCD enabled a total of 64 characters (or 2 to the 6th power). So, for example, the computer could distinguish between upper and lower case. Thus the first text processing computers adopted the BCD Coding system for text and continued to use the inherent binary coding system (Base 2) for the purpose of making calculations and processing the mathematical.

And this is how the processing of the textual began on the early computers. An additional layer of coding was added to the computer's circuitry to permit the translation of alphabetic characters. It still came down to the binary to be processed, but text information did not follow the same circuitry to be processed as did the mathematical. Electricity coded in binary for the nonmathematical was not merged with other binary-coded electricity as is the case when the computer does mathematical calculations. Circuitry was added to translate the binary code for the characters on input and on output.

When you think about it, applications like word-processors are basically text-in and text-out systems. Circuitry was essentially added in between the input circuit paths and the output circuit paths of the computer to accommodate binary-to-text translation-and the reverse, text-to-binary translation. This is what it took to get the early computers to process the textual.

As the computer evolved and more uses or applications were developed, the BCD coding system, like its predecessor Baudot, became inadequate. Many special characters were not defined in BCD. Characters like the copyright symbol (©) and the tilde symbol (~) were not included in BCD. Special function keys which today are taken for granted on a computer keyboard did not exist in the early days.

Eventually it became obvious that the now budding computer industry needed a new coding system for the processing of textual information. Or should I now say, "non-mathematical" information?

Given the precedents with Baudot and BCD, it didn't take a rocket scientist to see what direction the developers of this new coding system were destined to go. Also given the inherent 'binary' nature of the computer, that is, the need for the computer to have anything and everything in binary form in order to process, one could easily see that they were going to simply expand upon BCD.

And indeed this is what they did. They expanded the BCD code to provide 8 BITs for every character, special character and/or function key. By expanding the code to 8 BITs, we now had a coding system that could provide 256 unique codes. (If you take the Base of 2 and the exponent of 8 you get a result of 256 total possible combinations.) This total was more than enough to encompass the alphabet in upper-case as well as lower-case (26 letters times 2 for upper and lower case = 52) with a remainder of 204 codes to be used for unique characters or function key codes. This code was named EBCDIC. Extended Binary Coded Decimal Information Code.

The EBCDIC Code was actually created by a team of developers formulated by computer manufacturers of the time. You may surmise that UNIVAC, a company started by Mauchley & Eckert, the folks behind the very first ENIAC computer and IBM were major players in this effort. And the EBCDIC Code became standard implementations on all of their computers.

You may think that because they had over 200 possible unique characters remaining after completing the alphabet in both upper and lower case that this coding system would hold up forever. You are right! It has been holding ever since its inception. That's a long time!

But you should know that today EBCDIC has evolved to become identified with the bigger, not necessarily faster, and most definitely more expensive mainframe computers. In the early days, several manufacturers jumped into the budding computer marketplace. They all made "Big" computers that cost millions of dollars and required large rooms with specialized environmental controls, like air conditioning and dust control.

A friend of mine from way back when I was just getting started in teaching computers and computer literacy would refer to these computer manufacturers in this way. He would say "you have got IBM and then you have the BUNCH". "BUNCH" stood for Burroughs, UNIVAC, NCR, Control Data and Honeywell. And they all implemented the now defined 8-BIT EBCDIC Code. This became known as the 8-BIT Architecture.

EBCDIC for the non-mathematical and raw, pure, straight binary for the mathematical. That worked well then and continues to work well today. At least it does with the present day version of the IBM mainframe. However, many technical improvements across the board have been integrated over the years into the mainframe operating environment.

If I may digress a little here, the "BUNCH" is no longer a reality. Burroughs eventually merged with what became Sperry-UNIVAC to become a company known as UNISYS. NCR, short for National Cash Register, is still in business after being bought out by AT&T. AT&T thought they should be making computers. AT & T changed their minds and in 1996 spun off the NCR Division to be on its own again. NCR still makes great cash registers but its position in the computer marketplace today is unclear. Control Data migrated from making computers in the hardware sense into becoming a major player in the software and computer support related industries. And finally, Honeywell became a leader through the 70's in computer manufacturing only to be merged with Bull of Europe to become Honeywell-Bull in the 90's. Honeywell-Bull is no longer a significant player in the domestic U.S. mainframe market.

As you can see, much has changed over the years. And the first major change in the computer marketplace occurred in the mid-sixties. This is when Ken Olsen, formerly of IBM, developed a technique for making smaller computers that could process just as fast or even faster then the mainframes of the day. The IBMer executives, as the story goes, dismissed his computer design concepts as being impractical.

So Olsen started his own company. Today that company is known as Digital Equipment Corporation, or DEC for short. DEC hit the marketplace with computers that became known as "Mini-computers". DEC developed the VAX and VAX Cluster computers which became known as "Super-mini" computers.

The mini-computer market steadily grew up through the late eighties. DEC itself in 1988 was, based on revenue, the second largest computer manufacturer in the world, second only to IBM. What contributed to DEC's success is that they made smaller, cheaper, and BIT-for-BIT faster computers. One major element of the DEC minicomputers was the use of a character coding system using only 7-BITs per precoded character.

DEC developed and implemented a 7-BIT coding system for non-mathematical processing. Thats right. A 7-BIT code. Ken Olsen essentially said that a "Big" mainframe for all computer processing was not needed.

By researching uses of the EBCDIC coding system, it was learned that for the most part the 8-BIT coding system added cost and size to the manufacturing process of the computer. And a large percentage of the available codes left after encoding the alphabet upper & lower case and all special characters and functions were never used. Use them or lose them. If they are not needed, why manufacture the computer to have them?

This was the beginning of the end for Big computers in America. At last we learn that the computer does not have to be a big computer. So, what of this 7-BIT coding system for the non-mathematical?

It became known as the American Standard Code for Information Interchange or ASCII for short. It caught on quickly. It was the major force behind redesign of the "mainframe" computer in terms of its physical size and method of processing information at the machine level. Both were chief elements driving competition with Number One IBM.

All of the BUNCH during their day, eventually converted their computer mainframe manufacturing product lines to produce ASCII compliant computers with the 7-BIT architecture to process non-mathematical, that is "textual" information. As a result, physical size of the computer began to shrink because the computer running the 7-BIT architecture did not require as much hardware circuitry.

The BIT and De Facto Standardization

Knowing the computer is to know the "BIT". Knowing the "BIT" is of major importance to the student of the computer. The previous pages have given you the essential background on the inception, deployment and continuing evolution of the "BIT".

The media says continuously that new computer developments are isolated individual late-breaking inventions that are reshaping the way society processes information. But the reality of it is that we have come up with new and improved ways of "pushing" as I like to say, ...the "BIT". Smaller, cheaper faster and presumably better. The SCFB paradox continues to evolve. And will continue into the 21st century.

Among the many reasons why you need to know the BIT, is that in the evolution of the computer over the past 50 years, we have de facto standardized the way we define and express computer and computer network transmission rates. Terms like "32-BIT Processor" and a "BUS Size of 64-BITs" have become commonplace in characterizing the latest personal computers (PCs) and you need to know about these as well. However topics like "Bandwidth" and "Throughput" which are conveyed in terms of the number of BITs-per-second (bps) which can be transferred in any given second have become essential selling points in servicing and selling computer networks.

Companies from AT & T all the way down to the smallest local exchange company in America predicate their computer network services based on the number of BITs- per-second that can be transmitted. Executives managing large corporate network infrastructures and even an individual at home leasing an Internet account are faced with, whether or not they know it, the need to ensure that they have adequate "BIT" transmission rates in place to support their purchased or leased computer network services. You have heard the saying 'Time is Money'. Computer network services bear this saying out to the tangible reality. Time is truly money on a computer network. And it is measured in BITs-per-second.

The following acronyms have evolved in de facto style to signify the BIT rates used by the various network service companies. De facto means that these definitions were hurled upon us by propagation and use in the industry, business, commerce, and as such, made their way into our culture through the retail computer stores and the media.

There was never, to my knowledge, a standards committee commissioned to define BIT transmission rates.

So here they are, (see following) and you can now derive new meaning from your modem, and if applicable, your high speed network interface. Soon you will hear more about bps. The cable companies are positioned to roll out their new 'cable modem' products and services. Other local exchange companies are coming out with new technology this year to offer the consumer in the home higher bandwidth options which surpass those available via today's conventional modem. These new technologies will have much higher throughput rates measured in bps.

Standardized Abbreviations for BIT Transmission Rates

bps	BITs-per-second
Kbps	Kilo, or Thousand-BITs-per-second
Mbps	Mega, or Million-BITs-per-second
Gbps	Giga, or Billion-BITs-per-second
Tbps	Tera, or Trillion-BITs-per-second

Why do you need to know the "BIT"? Perhaps the above table is the key. I say this because not only do the networking companies predicate their service offerings based on how many BITs-per-second you are using, requesting or demanding to support your computer network needs. These companies actually bill you based on the "BIT transmission rate". This rate is expressed in BITs-per-second, as illustrated in the above table.

Common terms like 'Bandwidth' and 'Throughput' are measured in BITs-per-second (bps). And these types of computer terms need to be understood by companies and consumers alike as we continue to expand and connect over various computer networks.

In 1998, Vice-President Al Gore gave a press conference at which he explained that the new Internet will be able to transmit the entire

Encyclopedia Brittanica, some 30 very thick books, over the Internet in one second. That is, one second! It would have been more accurate and realistic for him to give us a bps rating, like 100Mbps. But most folks would not have comprehended that. Most people can identify with the thirty volumes of the Encyclopedia Brittanica. Just to make sure viewers could make this association, they had a table in front of the Vice-President during the news conference. Guess what was stacked up on the table?...you guessed it...all thirty volumes of the Encyclopedia Brittanica.

The thirty volumes actually caused some diversion from the real purpose of the Vice-President's speech, which was to reveal that a few companies got together with the government and contributed money and other resources to modify the existing Internet and create a new public Internet/World Wide WEB. This new Internet is now being called Internet II.

Because of the congestion and slowness of the current Internet/World Wide WEB, Mr. Gore referred jokingly to it as "the World Wide Wait". This slowness, however, relates directly to the BITs-per-second throughput capability of this network.

More and more folks are subscribing to this network. But the bandwidth and throughput, as measured in BITs-per-second have not been significantly changed since its inception. As a result, the increased user traffic being added is causing delays and congestion. At times it feels like the Los Angeles freeway or the capitol beltway surrounding Washington, D.C.!

But there are other reasons for knowing the "BIT". Other important components of the computer are measured in BIT form. Components like the Non-Mathematical Coding Systems we discussed. How many BITs for example does it take to process the letter 'A' in EBCDIC versus ASCII? Believe it or not, this becomes an important consideration, especially when you are paying to transmit perhaps in excess of millions of BITs per second (Mbps). Because letters in EBCDIC take 1 BIT more than ASCII to transmit.

Furthermore, modern day computers are evolving with new and improved techniques, and no matter what these techniques may be, it all must ultimately come down to binary. Remember, binary means, you guessed it—"BITs". So, if you understand this you can relate it to any new techniques and to what the true value is of the computer you may be thinking about purchasing.

3

The BIT, The First Computer and Evolving Computer Technology

Although there are several different versions of when and who invented the very first computer, we must begin somewhere in order to explain BITs. Many techno-historians would say that Atanasoff and Berry proved the theory of making calculations using symbolically coded electricity with their ABC computing machine in 1938. It became known as the ABC machine. Although the ABC machine proved the theory that the binary numbering system could be applied to the coding of electricity, it was not set up for production operation.

However, what the ABC machine proved in 1938 was applied to the building of a new machine. This machine was called the ENIAC. The ENIAC was completed by Mauchly and Eckert in years 1943-46. The acronymic name stands for Electronic Numerical Integrated Automatic Computer.

The ENIAC applied the theory of binary coded electricity. After completing its prototype testing, the ENIAC was used initially by the U.S. Army in calculating projectile trajectory paths. Security, you can imagine at that time, was super sensitive, because America was involved in World War II.

Yes, the computer had its origin in numerical calculations. It may have even been called 'computer'. But its main purpose in life was to do mathematical calculations. The computer evolved from a calculator.

The ENIAC, though, filled up the space required of two large rooms and required 18,000 vacuum tubes to operate. Nothing like the hand-held calculators of today. But the ENIAC is the computer that most technology observers will recognize as the very first.

The main purpose for each and every one of the 18,000 vacuum tubes in the ENIAC was to hold what is known today as an "ON" state or to be in an "OFF" state. One "ON" or "OFF" vacuum tube alone didn't amount to much. But when you take a series of 4, 6 or 8 vacuum tubes, in some combination of "ON" and/or "OFF" states, you could then apply "Binary Coding" which is based on the digits one(1) and zero(0) in order to make calculations. It is the binary numbering system in combination with the vacuum tubes that provided the foundation for what we know today to be the "Digital Computer". Furthermore when you apply the binary numbering system to 18,000 vacuum tubes, the calculating power becomes enormous.

Many folks are not predisposed to mathematical numbering systems let alone binary coding. I will therefore clarify what we mean by the binary numbering system. It is the primary numbering system which is at the heart of the technology which enables digital computers to process mathematical calculations.

It is also the numbering system upon which other computer coding systems are based. These other coding systems enable the numerous other uses of the computer which are non-mathematical such as creating a word-processing document or sendng an electronic mail message.

In other words, if it were mathematical, the early-day computers could calculate with it using the Base 2 or binary equivalent numbers. Base 2 numbers strictly use ones and zeroes to process. Electricity is "ON" or "OFF". Or, in the case of modern day computer network transmission, "ON" and "OFF" states are converted prior to going over the network to "HIGH" and "LOW" pulses. The pulses are converted back to "ON" or "OFF" states upon reaching their destination on the network.

With the inception of the first computer, scientists used ones and zeroes to represent the "ON" and "OFF" electrical states respectively of the numerical calculations to be processed. The vacuum tubes used in the calculation phase were set with switchboard-like plugs to program the ENIAC for the calculation. Pushing the plug into the vacuum tube equalled a one or an "ON" BIT. Pulling the plug out of the vacuum tube set the tube as a zero or an "OFF" BIT. After all of the BITs in the calculation program were set, electrical power was switched on and permitted to flow through the preset vacuum tube architecture of the ENIAC.

After the electricity flowed through this arrangement of tubes used in the calculation phase, new electrical current resulting from this movement of electricity through the preset tubes would result. The resulting current represented the answer to the calculation in pure electrical current form. In order to translate this pure electrical current, the ENIAC had to channel the current into a different section of vacuum tubes where no presetting had yet occurred. The result of doing this left this section of tubes in a certain state of ON and OFF tubes. This BIT state of affairs represented the anwer to the problem in binary. Scientists on the ENIAC then had to convert this binary representation into Base 10 manually for it to be understood by the ordinary person.

Remember that Base 10 is the numbering system we all know, love and use every day. Our U.S. system of currency is Base 10. Ten pennies make a dime. Ten dimes make a dollar and so forth. And Base 2 is binary. Base 2 has only 2 digits, the one and the zero. ON and OFF states are represented by 1 and zero respectively.

Although not a consideration at the time of the ENIAC, in computer networking, HIGH and LOW pulses are represented by 1 and 0 respectively. This is at the core of how digital computers, like the ones we use, can connect over networks to other computers located here, there and everywhere. Their respective base languages correlate via the binary numbering system. With electrical systems it's ON and OFF states. With laser light, radio and other network signalling systems it's HIGH and LOW pulse codes respectively. And it's binary 1s and 0s that bring it all together.

The BIT and Evolving Computer Technology

Since the ENIAC, the technology has evolved from vacuum tubes to transistors, then semi-conductors and integrated circuits working with super-improved transistor technology. Smaller, cheaper, faster, better! No longer impeded by the complications associated with operating a computer with 18,000 vacuum tubes, computers have become much more powerful and much cheaper and easier to operate. But computers today still fundamentally use Base 2 or the binary numbering system to represent BITs at the machine level and process information at nearly the speed of light.

Besides the varied improvements made in the technology to process and store "BITs" and the 1000s of different software packages that can now run on computers, some of the main differences between the early computers and modern day computers follow.

Today you don't really see that "BITs" are being processed, because there are no vacuum tubes. You don't see blinking lights as I did in the "Babes in Toyland" movie. By the way, the blinking lights you may surmise at this point, was the early computer's way of indicating the "ON" and "OFF" state of the "BITs" being processed. "ON" light equalled an "ON" BIT represented by a '1' or as we say, a "BIT 1". 'OFF' light equalled an 'OFF' BIT represented by a '0' or, as we say, a "BIT 0".

Comparing Early Day and Modern Day Computers

EARLY COMPUTERS	MODERN DAY COMPUTERS
Vacuum Tubes	Very Large Scale Integrated Circuits
Expensive (million - multi-millions)	BIT for BYTE Much Cheaper (hundreds - thousands)
Fast(miliseconds)	Super Fast (picoseconds)
Limited to Calculation:	Multi-Dimensional, Feature-Rich, Text/Graphics
Physically Large	Physically Small (Desktop/Hand-Held)
Specialized Operation	Easy-to-Use Operation
Binary Language Only	Binary Required, Many Other Languages
Interface Through Vacuum Tube	Graphical User Interface (GUI), Mouse, Keyboard
Stand-Alone (i.e. Not Connected On Network)	Comes with MODEM, Network Card
Deployed in the Computer Room	Deployed Everywhere

The first generation of computers to follow the ENIAC and subsequent generations up until the inception of the desktop computers were manufactured with light panels. In my earlier example from the "Babes In Toyland" movie, the blinking lights in the center box was intended by the movies' producers to be somewhat of an analogy to the vacuum tube operation of the first computers. That is, behind each light was a circuit, each light in the row was either "ON" or 'OFF' at any particular time to represent the "ON" and 'OFF' BITs being processed.

Computer technology has come a long way since the vacuum tube concept. Many volumes of text would be needed just to summarize all of the improvements over the past 50 years. And this task would take us beyond the scope of this particular book. My intention is to give you the major staples of the computer so that you can relate to any particular aspect of the computer or the computer network. To accomplish this you need first to know the BIT. Because no matter what the application is, everything on the computer or the computer network ultimately comes down to the BIT.

It was the BIT that was at the heart of the early compatibility problems that we experienced with computers. IBM and a few other companies who followed IBM directly, remained fully EBCDIC and continued to make large multi-million dollar mainframes. And herein lies the core of the problem which became known as the "compatibility" issue. And it was a "BIT" issue pertaining to how the computer processed the nonmathematical information, that is to say, character-based textual information.

During the seventies and eighties, many "would be" computer system buyers in the business world were required to ensure that the computer to be purchased was "compatible" with the software currently running on the company's computer or the software about to be purchased by the company. It was commonly known in the business that IBM sold only software that was compatible with its large mainframes, that is, 8-BIT EBCDIC encoded software.

During the eighties, before IBM began shifting its computer designs to be interoperable, some companies jumped into the marketplace with devices known as "protocol converters". Protocol converters were at the time hardware boxes, which could be used to make 8-BIT architectures compatible with 7-BIT architectures and vice-versa. It was not uncommon in those days for a company to have IBM mainframes running, with a "Protocol-Converter" connecting in DEC VAX super-minicomputers. The IBM mainframe essentially connected physically into one side of the protocol converter box and the DEC VAX connected into the other side. Information would flow in one side as 8-BIT and come out the other side as 7-BIT.

Many 7-BIT and 8-BIT spin-off products were developed around the incompatibilities associated with the computers made by what was then the number 1 and number 2 computer manufacturers in the world. Many forms of the "Protocol converter" were developed: like compression devices that improved 7-and 8-BIT-stream transmission, storage devices and monitors that could display an IBM mainframe (8-BIT) computer's current operations as well as the current operations of the DEC VAX (7-BIT) minicomputer.

All the while that these 2 computer manufacturers dominated the computer marketplace, 8-BIT and 7-BIT though they may have been, other companies and entrepreneurs continued to ask the fundamental question, "Do all computers have to be big and expensive?"

In as much as the vacuum-tube less computer at this time came in 2 sizes, mainframe and mini-computer. The mainframe required the space of one medium size room to contain the computer itself and all of its associated hardware. And the minicomputer which came in several sizes ranging from the space required for a large sofa down to the size of a modern day electric dishwasher. If anything at the time foretold the destiny of computer cost and size, it was the minicomputer. That is, the computer was destined to become smaller, cheaper, faster and better.

While the minicomputer enjoyed heavy sales in the face of continuing growth in the mainframe marketplace, the social impression of computers was that they were here to stay. Computer hardware was getting physically smaller. Eventually toward the late seventies, the first PCs called "Microcomputers" began to hit the marketplace. Apple and IBM became the leading manufacturers, at least throughout the eighties. Although Apple and IBM PCs were both very popular they were to remain largely incompatible in terms of BIT design architecture and type of software that each supported—well into the 90's. However, today many of the incompatibility issues have been replaced by the industry's drive to make computer systems "Open" or 'Interoperable'.

There are still incompatibilities. But these are more clearly known to consumers on purchase. For instance, the major incompatibility in the PC marketplace would be between the IBM, including clone and compatible PCs like those from DELL and COMPAQ, and the Apple/Macintosh line of computers. These two distinct lines of computers have at the most fundamental level, different architectures and Operating Systems software. This means the application software you buy translates BITs according to their respective hardware and operating system. Therefore when you buy software make sure you select the package that is compatible with your computer and operating system. All software is labeled as to what kind of computer(s) on which it will run.

The BIT and the Personal Computer

As smaller computers were deployed across America, good old American initiative sparked the demand for and the development of the technology necessary to continue to reduce the physical size and cost while improving the value of the computer. What followed was the inception of the microcomputer.

Needless to say, the early non-IBM microcomputers, being much smaller than the minicomputer, utilized a 7-BIT architecture. In the mid-to-late seventies the technology for the first "microcomputer" was in place. Inception began in the late seventies and the industry was on its way to putting a computer in front of the ordinary individual person.

Although there were a few other "first" microcomputers, society and the media will recall the very first Apple computer (circa 1979) as the first 7-BIT microcomputer. It took up the space of about one foot square on a table or desk and had the performance capacity sixteen times greater than the ENIAC. Needless to say, it did not require two full-size rooms, nor did it require or generate the heat of 18,000 vacuum tubes. It simply operated on normal house current.

And it took off like gangbusters. The Apple IIE led to the Apple IIC and many other revisions, all 7-BIT architectures building upon the Apple design concept. Perhaps most noteworthy is the inception of the Apple Macintosh line of computers. Throughout the 80's, the Macs, as they were called, evolved through many successive and successful variations. Each variation was a more powerful revision of the Apple computers that had come before it.

Furthermore, we had the Atari, Commodore, and others. Texas Instruments in the early 80's marketed a $25 computer that you could hold in one hand. It was the forerunner of today's much more powerful Palm Top computer, and Radio Shack came out with the TRS-80 line, which had a fairly decent run over the years.

Seeing the threat to its vital mainframe market, numero uno, IBM, reluctantly followed with the deployment of the IBM Personal Computer in 1981. It was a microcomputer based on the 8-BIT EBCDIC architecture. Since IBM already had their foot in the door with so many companies and because IBM had sold them mainframe computers for their enterprise, that is, corporate level computer needs, it was almost effortless for IBM to market their personal computers.

The IBM PC evolved to 286, the 386. Then the PS/2 line of computers, all like the Apple line, building and extending the original PC design concept. Designs which continued to utilize the 8-BIT EBCDIC architecture. The counterparts to the previous "mainframe-era" non-IBM manufacturers evolved with what was to become know as the "IBM Clone". And with this, the term "PC" became universally associated with any computer used by the individual, regardless of whether the computer was on the desktop or used on the person's lap, and regardless of who manufactured the computer.

Throughout the eighties, companies like COMPAQ, Packard-Bell and DELL made cheaper clones of the early IBM PC line of computers. Several of these non-IBM companies got together and standardized on the specifications for the PC computer utilizing the ASCII-7 BIT architecture. Eventually IBM was to follow these standard specifications in making their PCs.

By 1990 everyone was making PCs. The ASCII-7 BIT character set was now a standard ingredient on most PCs. And the other essential components needed to make a PC like the processor chips and memory chips became major marketable items because of their evolving and increasing speed and capacity to process BITs.

The PC market enjoyed phenomenal growth throughout the eighties and nineties. Today IBM has the Aptiva line of PCs and many other innovative developments. But the interesting thing about the PC market is that COMPAQ Computer forged ahead as #1 in market share in the PC marketplace back in 1995. And COMPAQ has remained number one since that time.

COMPAQ bought Digital Equipment (DEC), former #2, in 1998. This acquisition illustrates the direction of the computer marketplace. And given that DEC's inception was with mini-computers in the 60's, and COMPAQ's inception was with PCs in the 80's, you can see that this deal is another clear example of the marketplace moving ever so quickly toward smaller, cheaper, faster and presumably better technology.

The PC took off internationally as well. Overcoming the language barrier became the next "non-mathematical" encoding hurdle. But it didn't take very long. The industry developed something called "UNICODE". This is a multi-lingual extension of both the ASCII and EBCDIC codes. These coding systems were extended by appending '16-BIT' circuitry to the standard ASCII and EBCDIC '8-BIT' character sets.

You may recall that standard ASCII and EBCDIC are 7-BIT and 8-BIT coding systems. UNICODE 'redevelops' ASCII and EBCDIC onto a 16-BIT format, such that all the BITs above 8 essentially are null values or zeroes for the corresponding ASCII and EBCDIC characters. The remaining BIT positions in UNICODE are used to encode the character sets of all of the remaining languages of the world, including those languages which are 'phonetic' or sound-based, such as Chinese. Many of these characters actually need between eight and sixteen BITs in order to encode in binary form.

Since each character of every language requires its own unique binary code, you can appreciate why UNICODE would need to be 16-BIT. With an 8-BIT character coding system, there is a total maximum number of 256 unique 8-BIT binary codes. That is two to the eighth power. With UNICODE there are 2 to the 16th power number of unique binary codes. This is a total of 65,536 unique 16-BIT binary character codes. Enough for all of the characters in ASCII and EBCDIC, as well as all the languages of the world.

The UNICODE character set is now being manufactured into computers all around the world. Imagine creating an e-mail message in any language, or having your computer translate volumes of written works in any language!

The foregoing examples are a preview of the direction computer technology could take to bring the peoples of the world together. Just think of this concept being applied to the telephone or even the videophone. Divergent cultures at last being able to communicate on a real-time basis. It is these types of developments that cause me to reflect back on the "Babes In Toyland" movie with continuing wonderment.

4

The BIT Today As A Major Power Influence

The "Data BUS" is the part of the computer which is like the "main highway" for all of the BITs which are processed through the computer. It is unclear to me how we arrived at the name "Data BUS". However the term has emerged as one of the most critical "power factors" in measuring the power of any computer.

Imagine for a moment a desktop computer. Now take the monitor and place it off to the side. Typically, what the monitor sits on is the box we refer to as the processor box or the system box. There are other names, as well, but I think you get the point. Look at the processor box from above the desk or table on which it may be sitting. What you will find, generally, is that the box is about one foot square (although this size is getting smaller).

Now if we remove the cabinet cover from the processor box and place it to the side, we will see a bunch of slots for other add-on circuit boards. These are called "expansion slots". We can see some smaller cabinets that house other components. There also would be a few bundles of wire. Continuing to look at the bare insides of the processor box from directly above the unit face down, we would see a main board of typically greenish color which is approximately one foot square and buried under all of the other components.

Even though smothered by all of the other components, we would see through some of the gaps that this main board has circuits etched into it. Computer engineers call these 'traces'. These circuits are actually hardwired and embedded into the main board. Circuits going everywhere! Moreover, if we studied it long enough we would actually begin to see that everything that has to do with the computer, and I do mean everything, is in some way connected into this main board.

This "main board" is generally referred to as the "Motherboard". On the larger mainframe computers and on the older mini-computers and today's "mid-range" computers, this board is called the "backplane". The reason why this board is characterized as the "main" board is because in addition to everything inside connecting into it, all other devices outside the box, like printers and keyboards, connect to the motherboard as well.

And not only does the board provide a connection, physically, for all of the other computer components, but BIT processing occurs through the board's etched-in circuitry or 'traces' if you will. And processing occurs in the form of what they call "BIT Stream Transfers". That is, bazillions of BITs being processed from their source component (say,the keyboard)and sent on to their next destination component (say, the computer's Main Memory or the Monitor Display). So, the Data BUS is like a "circuit highway for BITs" carved onto the Motherboard's surface. And the Data BUS provides connectivity for BIT transfer purposes for all of the components connected inside and outside of the processor box.

The size of the Data BUS is a critical power factor in any computer. The motherboard may generally be about one foot square. However the size of the Data BUS is never the same size as the motherboard. It can be much smaller. Remember, the motherboard has to fit inside of the processor box.

The Data BUS is circuitry which is carved out on the actual motherboard. You can surmise, then, that the Data BUS is going to always be physically smaller than the motherboard. Then how, you may be asking yourself, do we measure the size of the Data BUS.

We measure the size of the Data BUS based upon the number of BITs it can process, not the physical dimensions of its hosting motherboard. The first personal computers all were manufactured with an 8-BIT Data BUS. This meant that only 8 BITs could be transferred over the Data BUS at any moment in time. Computer "moments " are typically measured at the micro-second and nano-second level. That is a millionth-of-a-second and a billionth-of-a-second respectively.

Since the first PCs, the size of the Data BUS has grown to 16-BIT, 32-BIT and 64-BIT. Today most PCs have either a 32-or 64-BIT Data BUS. Now the growth in Data BUS size may not seem like a whole lot of difference. But you need to consider the fact that computers work on electricity. This means computers are super fast devices in their operations! However the difference between a computer with an 8-BIT Data Bus and a computer with a 64-BIT Data BUS is illustrated by the analogy to an 8-lane highway and a 64-lane highway respectively.

And even the difference between an 8-lane and a 64-lane highway, although hard to imagine in our gridlock society, does not seem to push our size-imagination limits into outer space. However, the real difference in processing speed is enormous. Cars run on gasoline and are measured in miles. One mile is 5,280 feet. Computers run on electricity and are measured in BITs.

The fastest typical gas-powered cars are somewhere in the range between 200-300 miles-per-hour. The land record for a car is now over 600mph. (But this is an exception.) Electricity travels at 186,000 miles-per-second. That is 11,160,000 miles-per-minute or 669,600,000 miles-per-hour if you would like to put it on the same rating scale as the car. We measure distance inside the processor box in inches at the long-end and in nanometers at the short-end. A nanometer is one-billionth of a meter. Imagine traveling at several hundred million miles per hour inside a box which is only one foot square in size. Now imagine traveling at several hundred million miles per hour inside a semiconductor or an integrated circuit which is the size of a needle head. Actually it would now be smaller than a needle head. This is the kind of highway-environment on which BITs travel inside the computer.

Now imagine this kind of environment for "BIT-travel" if you will, with 32 or 64 lanes to travel on. The Data BUS is the total number of lanes or circuits available for transferring BITs. Is the picture becoming a little clearer? As you can see, distance and power need to be viewed under a completely different paradigm than what we humans are used to if we are to appreciate the enormous power of the computer.

The Data BUS is the most important BUS in the computer because all of the other computer components connect into the Data BUS. However, the term "Data BUS" is somewhat vague. This is because it is unclear how the name BUS originated and there are other types of BUSes.

Some of the other components which connect into the Data or Main BUS have their own BUS. For example, the monitor or visual display unit contains its own BUS. This BUS is called the "Video BUS". The Central Processing Unit (CPU) which is considered by many to be the "brains" of the computer has an "Address BUS". You could refer to the "Address BUS" as the "CPU BUS" because that is what it is.

Consequently, all of the sub-components in the CPU are connected via the "Address BUS". You can apply this analogy to the monitor and its "Video BUS as well. Essentially these other BUSes are lanes for BIT transfer within their respective component and in interfacing with the Main Data BUS. Incoming and outgoing BITs travel or transfer from the Main BUS into, say the monitor via the Video BUS. And likewise for the CPU and any other component with its own BUS which may be connected to the motherboard. The reverse is also true. That is, BITs from within these various components which have their own BUS travel out of the component via their respective BUS and onto the Main BUS enroute to their destination component.

So if you have ever wondered what magic was behind your document getting from your screen, which is actually also residing in main memory (if it is on your screen it is active in memory) to your disk, the above paragraph(s) describe the process. It is not magic at all. Basically, BITs are transferred to and from respective hardware components.

So if you ever have the opportunity to view an actual motherboard, keep in mind that when you see the numerous hardwired circuits which are etched into the motherboard, that a certain number of these circuits (i.e. 32 or 64 of them) will constitute the main Data BUS. The main Data BUS is always going to be visible because it is a required BUS.

Many other circuits will be visible. And many of these circuits may constitute other BUSes for this particular computer system. But these other BUSes are not necessarily required to be present. Some other BUS names include, but are not limited to: expansion BUS, local BUS, disk BUS, video BUS and memory BUS.

Lastly, keep in mind that there will be other required hardwire circuits on the motherboard which are not a part of any BUS. These type circuits are present to fulfill some ancillary or independent type of function which, although necessary, do not generally get included in describing the overall power of the computer.

Other techniques and fundamentals relate to the Data BUS, but most of these go beyond the scope of this book. Here I'm providing the essentials you need to know to understand the essential power of computer technology.

Another very important way of viewing BIT transfers is to explain how the BITs are actually moving across the Data BUS or any BUS. I often refer to this in my classes as viewing "BITs Across the Wire". A couple of things need to be considered first. How many wires are involved in the transfer? And how far does the transfer need to go?

If you have only a single circuit wire, than only 1 BIT at a time can travel on that wire. Now many other single BITs can follow behind that one BIT, but you can't group BITs, say in a group of 8, 16, 32 or 64 BITs in a single transfer. To do this you would require 8, 16, 32 or 64 circuit wires.

Now, if we are considering BIT transfers within the processor box, than it is quite likely that you have, in many cases, a multi-circuit hardwired Data BUS which could support transferring, say 32 or 64 BITs in a single group, at least along the main Data BUS.

But then how would the continuing transfer take place if the destination component happens to be a modem? A serial (modem) interface is constructed with only a single-wire input circuit to receive BIT transfers "one BIT at a time", off of the main Data BUS?

The answers to the above question can be found in the differences between serial and parallel BIT transfers. Serial BIT transfer occurs one BIT at a time. Indeed, serial means sequentially one at a time. And this is essentially what serial transfer is, one BIT at a time along a single-wire circuit. Now we already know that the size of the main Data BUS on modern day PCs is usually 32 or 64 BIT. This means 32 or 64 BITs can be grouped and transferred along a 32 or 64-wire circuit at the same time. So, one major distinction between serial and parallel BIT transfers is single-wire circuit versus multi-wire circuit, respectively.

Another dead give away between serial and parallel BIT transfers lies in the distance that the BIT transfer needs to cover. When we talk about the main Data BUS in the processor box of the computer, we are talking about a multi-wire circuit, which can easily handle group BIT transfers. Distance in this case is very short, and indeed is contained within a space on the motherboard that is smaller than one-foot square. In reality, the space is much smaller than one foot square, but the point is that the distance is such that we can economically provide the resources to engineer a multi-wire circuit.

Imagine if the distance was longer, say to a modem which connects your PC to another computer located 1,000 miles away. Can we economically provide for a multi-wire circuit to support the BIT transfers that will be needed? Not likely! Can you imagine running a 64-wire circuit for 1,000 miles? That is why single-wire or serial interfaces are used. In fact, in this modem example, the BIT transfer begins over the main Data BUS on the computer in parallel transfer mode with the destination component being the modem.

The modem has a serial transfer interface connection to the Main Data BUS. This means that the BIT transfer from the main Data BUS that is parallel is converted to serial transfer when it goes through to the modem. The modem is a serial device with a single-wire, serial input. So the modem organizes the parallel BIT transfer coming in from the computer's main Data BUS. The BIT transfer then continues on through the modem in serial BIT transfer mode and then out and onto a pre-existing phone line which is a BIT serial transfer circuit. At the other end where the remote computer is located the process is simply completed in reverse order. The remote modem converts from incoming serial BIT transfer onto the main Data BUS of the remote computer in BIT parallel transfer mode.

I said that Serial BIT transfers occur one BIT at a time over a single wire. From this you might surmise that the grouping of BIT s could not take place in serial transfers. In fact BIT groupings do occur with serial transfers. And BIT groupings do occur on non-parallel circuits. However, serial BIT transfer groupings occur in a manner in which all of the BITs in the group travel 1-BIT at a time, beginning with a "Start BIT" to mark the beginning of the BIT group and followed by the BITs in the group one BIT at a time, each BIT following the BIT "in front of it" in a sequential manner with the last BIT in the group typically being a "Stop BIT". Stop BITs mark the end of a BIT grouping in serial BIT transfers. This is how it is done for a typical modem based BIT transfer.

What changes in other serial transfers is the BIT size of the group. In larger serial transfers these include source and destination address as well as protocol type. This is the stuff of which network engineers are made! I won't take you there just yet, but suffice it to say that large BIT groupings today are what support much of high-speed networking across the country. When I say "large", I mean in the millions of BITs-per-second range and above.

Parallel BIT transfers, on the other hand, transfer the entire group of BITs at the same time. As a result, parallel BIT transfers are much faster because all BITs in the grouping are transferred at the same moment in time. All BITs in the group actually move in parallel not in sequence.

Many printers use a parallel interface to the main Data BUS of a computer. When you think about it, a printer is a device that is external to the processor box of the computer and is connected to the motherboard by a cable. In this case it is a "Parallel Printer Cable". This cable connects to the printer's parallel port and then to the corresponding port on the processor box, which is ultimately connected into the motherboard. Unlike the modem example above, which involves a BIT parallel to BIT serial conversion during BIT transfer, this printer example would be a parallel-to-parallel BIT transfer.

Now you can have serial printers as well. In fact, modern day computer systems and computer networks have a mixture of BIT serial and BIT parallel devices. There are numerous examples of devices, which use BIT serial or BIT parallel transfer. From modems and printers on up to systems like "Massively Parallel Processors". To describe all of these devices goes beyond the scope of this book.

You do not need to know about all of these various devices to understand the basic differences between BIT serial and BIT parallel transfer. But the main Data BUS is always BIT parallel. And PC modems are usually BIT serial. (This changes with the inception of cable modems in 1999) These are important constants to keep in mind.

Finally, it is useful to understand that devices connecting into the main Data BUS may be either BIT parallel or BIT serial. And the device to be connected would require its respective type of cable (i.e. serial or parallel cable). Or, if it is a 'wireless' device, it usually will require a hardware component to be added in a slot or otherwise connect into the motherboard.

In the next chapter we will discuss in more detail the computer's speed. A computer's processing speed is a function of the size of its main Data BUS. But the main Data BUS is not the only ingredient which makes up the computer's overall power and speed. Speed is also a function of how fast the computer can process electricity itself. For instance, how fast does the electrical current itself flow inside the computer? We refer to this as the computer's 'clock speed'.

The BIT and Clock Speed

We know that the electrical current going to an ordinary house in America flows at the rate of 60 cycles-per-second. Cycles-per-second is referred to as Hertz. No, not the rent-a-car company, but frequency as measured in cycles-per-second, named after the German physicist, Heinrich Hertz, who developed this method of measuring frequency.

Many folks dread the thought of having to consider or review mathematical concepts from high school, but I would like to take you back to good old algebra and trigonometry for just a brief moment. Remember when you studied trigonometric functions? The teacher would illustrate some of these trig functions using an X and a Y coordinate graph. The X would always be the horizontal line. The Y would always be the vertical line. The teacher then used this graph to further illustrate how each quadrant of the X-Y graph could be viewed as having 90 degrees, and that all 4 quadrants combined into a perfect circle equal to 360 degrees. This would lead then into discussions of how we could impose curves onto the X-Y graph and illustrate all or parts of the 360 degrees in a curved manner.

Given the above then I can introduce you to the fundamentals of how we measure and exploit the phenomenon of electricity. We measure the speed of electrical current in cycles-per-second. A complete cycle is equal to 360 degrees. How is that for simplicity?

You may be more comfortable with considering this as simply a sine wave. That is, similar to heart monitors, fetal monitors, etc. These devices use the sine wave to illustrate HIGH and LOW pulses which get translated to ON and OFF states inside the device and thus can be processed as BITs. When I explain this concept to my classes, I always ask "What would a flatline represent on a heart monitor?". Usually they get the picture. The most common answers are 'death' and 'zero' state.

Many devices are used today to monitor and manipulate electrical current. These devices illustrate on a scope the actual "modulation" of the electrical current. Heinrich Hertz discovered that electrical current could be categorized in successive levels from amplitude modulation, or the lower cycles-per-second on up to frequency modulation, and even higher ultra-high frequency modulation.

Hertz's work resulted in substantial improvements on the ways we use and deploy electricity. Now that we could measure electricity, we could control it. In his honor then, "cycles-per-second" became abbreviated as Hertz or 'Hz'. Everyone, for the most part today, uses Hz. However, generally speaking, only in the computer field do we use Hz to represent the computer's "clock speed". All the current computer ads will tout the clock speed of the computer using typically MHz. Or, the ads will capitalize all three letters as 'MHZ'. The MHz refers to the Megahertz level or "million-cycles-per-second. An important power factor!

Examples abound on ways in which Hertz's work can be illustrated. The one I cherish the most is that of a "fetal monitor". I was in the birthing room for all 4 of our children's births. I studied with keen interest the fetal monitor used in the room at each of my kid's deliveries. Most notable is the evolution from larger box to smaller, and the amount of detail provided on the panel display regarding the status of the yet-to-be-born child. There was a sine wave going real-time on the monitor's display screen. And there was quantitative information on things such as heartbeat and respiration being updated, also real-time. Each change in the sine wave had corresponding updates to the quantitative information displayed.

There are numerous types of monitors which illustrate the modulation of electrical current. And more importantly, I should say "coded electrical current", because each cycle of electrical current is one part of a pattern of cycles which, on the whole, result in the transmission of information, whether it be words, numbers, an image, images in motion with sound, like television or simply sound, as in radio.

As discussed, Hertz is abbreviated as Hz. So 1Hz would be one cycle-per-second of electricity. Now the electrical current going into a computer goes in at the rate of 60Hz. This is why you can plug a PC in at home and it works with no problem. You can plug in a radio, television or a lamp. These devices as well are rated for 60Hz. 60Hz is the standard in America for consumers. Sometimes you hear this as "It will run on 'Standard Household Current'". Standard household runs at 60Hz. And it also happens to be what is run everywhere in America by consumers and businesses that use electricity.

But unlike standard household appliances, there is something a little magical about what the computer does with its 60Hz of electrical input. And this is another of the characteristics like Data BUS size that determines the power of a computer. The computer takes the 60Hz of electrical input and steps it up to the millions of cycles-per-second level almost instantaneously. It does this through its transistorized circuitry.

The first computers did not do this because the phenomenon of the transistor had not yet been invented. The first computers ran on pure household current. That is, at 60Hz or 60 cycles-per-second.

Once the transistor was developed and deployed across the marketplace we had transistor radios and solid state television sets which replaced TVs running on vacuum tubes. It was during this period that the vacuum tubes which operated computers were replaced by the sensation of the century known as the "transistor".

The transistor enables the computer to take standard household current running at 60Hz and "step it up" to the "millions-of-cycles - per-second level. Or as we say today the "Megahertz Level". That is to say that the electrical current operating inside the processor box itself runs at the "Megahertz Level". And this has become known as the computer's "clock speed". And we represent Megahertz with the abbreviation MHz. Always upper case M and H followed by lower case z.

Clock speed, like the size of the main Data BUS is one of the most important power factors on the computer. The first IBM PCs, circa 1981, ran at a clock speed of 4MHz which was considered lightning fast back then. Over the past 15 years computer clock speed has continually evolved upward. Today the major computer manufacturers are tauting the latest PCs and Notebook computers running at 400MHz. Just five years ago, I recall that a computer running at

33MHz was considered among the fastest available. And we were all talking then about the new Pentium chip which was going to enable the PC to go over the 100MHz clock speed threshold. Current predictions are that we will have a 1GHz or 1 gigahertz clock speed computer by year 2000. Smaller, cheaper, faster, better!

In summary, what is important to understand about clock speed is that we are talking about how fast the electrical current moves inside the computer. The faster the clock speed, the more powerful the computer. In earlier chapters we discussed the "coding of electricity" as being integral to the whole operation of the computer. This is still true. Now with clock speed we introduce an element of computers that pertains to "how fast the coded electricity moves".

We humans are used to turning on the light and the light coming on instantly. There is no seeming delay in time. Therefore we learn that the turning on of the switch is the exact time that the light bulb activates and sheds its light in the room.

The fact is that there is a delay. Household current runs at 60Hz or 60 cycles-per-second. That is slow compared to the latest PCs' clock speed running at 400MHz, or million-cycles-per-second. But fast enough to lead us humans to think that there is no delay between the time we turn on the light switch and when we see the light come on. Now if it is that fast at 60Hz, can you imagine how fast the "coded-electricity" is running in a computer with a clock speed of 400MHz, or over 6 million times faster than the light bulb?

Lastly, clock speeds vary among components inside the processor box. But the one which I refer to above (i.e. 400MHz) and the one which advertisers tout, and the one you will encounter in the media, is actually the CPU or Processor Clock Speed.

The BIT and Size & Type of Instruction Set

The clock speed of the computer is a very important determinant of the power of the computer, because it relates directly to the computer's overall speed. Another important power factor determinant on the computer is the type of "Instruction Set" which is installed into the computer at the manufacturing plant. In fact, the clock speed, size of the main Data BUS and the type of instruction set together combine to affirm the rating characteristic known more commonly as "MIPS" for Millions of Instructions Per Second. Simply stated, the higher the MIPS rating the more powerful the computer.

Every action on the computer, generally speaking, can be traced to a unique "instruction" which is hardwired into the computer's circuitry. These instructions amount to commands basically which the computer performs on the BITs which are stored in chip-locations on the motherboard. The combined actions of "moving BITs" electrically among the various chip locations according to the respective instruction set commands is what enables the computer to not only calculate the mathematical as well as process the non-mathematical, but also give the impression that it (the computer) has intelligence.

Every computer must have an instruction set. And every action processed by the computer must "scan" this instruction set in order to be processed. The computer scans the entire instruction set until it finds the command that corresponds with the desired action. Let's say, for example, we were Adding two numbers. Assuming the numbers were already keyed in, upon pressing the "enter" key to signal the computer to Add the two numbers, a stream of "BITs" representing the "ADD" instruction in electrical pulse form is sent down the circuit from the keyboard to the computer's instruction set.

This BIT stream pulses through or scans the instruction set until it finds the instruction associated with the BIT-Binary equivalent of ADD. It actually is not complicated. You have a BIT Stream of On and Off codes in a certain order. That is, the order which represents the command, ADD. This ordered stream of BITs begins sequentially to compare itself with each instruction in the instruction set. When the exact comparison of the ordered BIT-stream is located on the Instruction Set, the computer directs the BIT stream into the circuitry associated with that instruction. The BIT stream then splits out according to the "Trace Circuits" hardwired there for processing an ADD Instruction. Pulse codes of on and off BITs then travel onward to the circuit(s) connecting the 2 registers where the two numbers are currently being stored in the binary coded electrical form. Here the circuit enables the 2 registers to merge one on top of the other. The result is straight binary arithmetic with the resulting calculation taking up residence in the first register involved with the calculation.

Over the years, the need for each command to scan the entire instruction set has been a major concern. Obviously it takes more time, even though completely electrical, to scan the entire instruction set versus, say, going directly to the Instruction needed at the moment. Research also supports the fact that over 80% of the instructions are never used in certain computer environments. That is, those environments doing largely mathematical calculations as they do in science and research environments. Now these are not simple mathematical calculations, like, "what is the probability of snow in the East?", or "what is your monthly payment on a $20,000 loan at 9% over a 15-

year term?" We are talking about calculations such as how long it would take for a spaceship from Earth to reach the planet Jupiter, have ample quantities of living space, air, fuel and food for four astronauts, and return to Earth through its atmosphere at the optimal entry point on one of several dates in an ideal range of dates during specific times on those dates!

As such, the speed of calculations in this type of environment became a concern. The computer industry's response initially was to manufacture computers, which had far less instructions hardwired into the computer's instruction set. With less instructions to scan, the theory goes, the faster the computer can process its actions within the domain of actions covered by its reduced instruction set. Obviously the computer still has to scan the entire instruction set on every action to be processed, but with a reduced number of instructions to scan, it will process that much more quickly. Such computers have become known as RISC Computers. RISC meaning Reduced Instruction Set Computers. (A sidenote here is that RISC computers generally cost more because they are somewhat of an exception to the computer mass production line. As such, special processes must be employed, versus the routine process setup on the regular line.)

The speed with which the computer can process these instructions has become a major power factor determinant because in many cases certain computers have been demonstrated as being able to process commands faster than humans have been able to make decisions. And this, indeed, has happened with modern day computers. I'm sure you all have heard about the famous Battle of Wits chess games that have been made popular in the media. Sometimes the computer wins, sometimes the Chess Master wins.

But what we must always remember, here, is that the computer will always have a finite set of instructions hardwired into it. The computer can master the game of chess, but when you think about it, chess has a finite number of possible moves. Humans do not have any limits in terms of how many instructions we can process. At least no limits have been proven. Some good inferences have been made. But the sky is still the limit for humans. If anything, humans will always be somewhat slower because of the human need to be thorough and exhaustive. Whereas the computer will always complete its latest command instruction even if that result is incorrect, incomplete or completely off the wall. If the instruction selected does not correlate with an instruction on the computer's instruction set, a system error will occur.

Also, remember that humans have emotions, something computers will never have. It is not possible to binarilize human emotions.

Much innovation has been going on for years in the area of improving the computer's instruction set. Because of the potential for chaos, the industry has standardized on what is known as the Complex Instruction Set for Computers, or CISC computer for short. CISC computers are the general standard for PCs and Notebook computers today. RISC computers are the exception and are deployed for uses, which have a justifiable need for reducing the instruction set scanning time in mathematical applications.

A new technology currently on the market in the latest PCs and Notebook computers is MMX. I would be remiss if I did not speak to this development which influences any current assessment of computer instruction sets. If you ask the computer store salesperson "What is MMX?", generally the answer will be something related to "Multi-media". Although related, MMX represents much more.

MMX technology came out in 1996. After a few problems and much debugging, the manufacturers were able to get it stabilized. Now in 1998 many computer manufacturers are touting their latest processors using MMX. MMX stands for **M**atrix **M**ath e**X**tensions.

What MMX does is extend and expand the power of the computer's instruction set by adding a set of 57 additional instructions and larger registers, specifically 8 each 64-BIT-Size registers onto the motherboard at the front-end of the processing cycle. These additional instructions and registers are built into the processor's circuitry. MMX does not replace the CISC instruction set technology. It enhances it.

In mathematical operations where 80% of the instructions are rarely used, it was a no-brainer to create a computer for dedicated mathematical operations to increase processing speed. In more current day applications, however, what was learned by analyzing usage patterns is that similar "BIT patterns" are processed when users need to do multi-media kinds of processing. That is, non-mathematical processing. Like RISC computers, in these types of applications of the computer, it was not necessary to scan the entire instruction set if the multi-media related commands could be processed and grouped at the front-end of the processing cycle.

So if the computer has MMX technology, this means that the computer has an additional 57 instructions and 8 each additional 64-BIT wide MMX registers, both of which are logically located at the front end of the processing cycles on the motherboard. If the software on this type of computer indicates that what is being processed is 'MMX related' the MMX technology kicks in, namely the instruction set with the 57 instructions versus the CISC instruction set. And whatever is being processed is "grouped" so that it can be swiftly processed through the 8 each 64-BIT registers versus the 8, 16 or 32-BIT registers which are universally located throughout the motherboard.

MMX technology, of course, for now, costs more because it requires more circuitry with the additional instruction set and 8 each 64-BIT registers. And I think you can see that the manufacture of a computer with MMX technology, like the RISC computers, has required "retooling" of the assembly line, so to speak. Many of the other very fine PCs and Notebooks currently on the market do not have MMX. You will observe a major price difference for now between MMX computers and all others. But even the MMX price will gradually come down over the next 2 years, because eventually most individual PC type of computers will run the MMX technology. This means that more people will buy them, which means more competition to sell them, which means the prices will come down.

Lastly, the relationship of the computer's instruction set to the computer's main Data BUS and the computer's clock speed is critical. These three factors combine to determine a major part of any computer's power and speed. Some analysts today think that prevailing clock speeds (i.e. 400MHz and growing) eliminate the problem of needing multiple or varying types of instruction sets. The rationale is that if you need to scan more instructions to operate, this is not a problem, because the computer, like the human brain, can scan at ultra-high rates of speed.

This is a valid point. Also, when you combine the added manufacturing costs of RISC and MMX computers, the argument gains momentum. However, as we expand our knowledge of the computer, we correspondingly expand our use, which results generally in more and newer ways (i.e. applications) of moving BITs & BYTEs. These result in improvements in both computer hardware and software technology, which then tends to lead to a demand for smaller, cheaper, faster and presumably better computer technology. Generally it all comes down to what you are trying to do with the computer, (i.e. applications) not the computer itself.

Furthermore computer technology will always have limits attached to it. So, today it is MMX with CISC for instruction set(s) running at 400MHz over a 64-BIT main Data BUS. These are still limits as awesome as we may want to perceive computer technology. That is to say that the clock speed and BUS size for example, will never be infinity, it will always have a cap. The cap may be the largest or the fastest heretofore, but nevertheless it will be bounded.

Memory

The fourth and final power factor, which I would like to mention here, briefly, is memory. That is, active, dynamic and volatile memory. It is where everything gets processed in and out of the computer. Displaying, saving to permanent storage, printing and transferring out over the network are among the many functions which begin in active main memory. It is clearly a major power influence.

However, memory is measured in BYTEs so I will cover that in detail in the next part of the book. I will mention here, that in simple terms, the more active memory you have onboard your computer, the faster it will run for you. And you can load up and keep active more programs at the same time.

Lastly, memory is a term that continues to evolve. At its inception into our culture back in the fifties, it was called primary storage. However, this term itself has evolved into something a little more complex. When ROM or Read-Only-Memory was developed as part of primary storage, scientists began to call what was active memory...RAM or Random Access Memory. RAM is still used today to identify active memory, particularly in radio and TV commercials, because it takes a few less milliseconds to say RAM versus memory on the air, which means more commercial time for the commercial buck.

As computer technology evolved and other memory functions were developed outside of primary storage, another term for active memory developed known as "Main Memory". This term is used still today, but much less frequently.

In my estimation, having evaluated the evolution of the technology for these past few decades, the most popular reference these days for active memory is simply 'memory'.

5

BIT Summary

Earlier I explained how executives would benefit by having a BIT-level appreciation for budgetary line items related to the corporation's computer and computer network purchases, or at least be able to ask BIT-based questions about such purchases. The strategic importance of this capability to the corporation's long-term information technology vision is inestimable. It gives the executive greater control over this aspect of the corporate budget. If you know the BIT then you can ask the right questions. If you know the BIT then you can understand the answers to such questions.

I wrote about how knowing the BIT would help you respond to questions from students and children, and not necessarily in computer science related subject areas alone. The computer and computer network now cuts across the entire curriculum as well as all aspects of society.

Teachers are now expected to be "computer literate". Executives and parents are being pulled in that direction by their families, even though, we, as a society, have still not come to a consensus on what 'computer literacy' means. President Bush, in 1993, was the first president of the United States to have a PC installed on his desktop.

The Year 2,000 (Y2K) issues which have been influencing information technology planning for the last several years, will continue to grow into a major area of concern for consumers as well as the manufacturers of the technology. Many of these Y2K issues are ostensibly computer or computer network BYTE related. But all BYTEs are made up of a varying number of BITs. Knowing the BIT will help you in understanding a large part of the Y2K set of problems now unfolding.

Speed and power are now identified as 'real time' critical factors in most corporate computing environments around the world. (I define 'real-time' as being able to respond to an information request at the time the request is made. That is, no procedural or other delays, immediate information satisfaction.) The BIT relates directly to the speed and power of the computer. These are also two of the most popular areas of discussion among students and other children because of the fascination factor.

Knowing the BIT enables adults to respond to questions and redirect well-intentioned efforts most appropriately, in a supportive and accurate manner. This is truer today than ever before, what with the Internet and World Wide WEB being connected directly to all schools and with the push on to get family homes on-line.

And it is the networking of computers into the schools as well as corporate America and the home which has fostered enormous growth in information technology over the past 10 years. Small networks now must connect to larger networks which must connect to still larger networks. The Internet and World Wide WEB are good examples.

Most companies have their own proprietary networks, with connections to the Internet and World Wide WEB. Designing and maintaining computer network infrastructures has become a major cost factor to companies and a major requirement in order to do business in today's global marketplace.

Many important BIT-related characteristics have made their way into our culture, particularly through the media. Buying and understanding a computer today necessitates an understanding of the BIT. Elements like bandwidth and throughput as expressed in BITs-per-second(bps), are used frequently in evaluating the performance of computers and computer networks. And I refer to a network in the corporate, educational, and or family home environment. Knowing the BIT means that you will be able to manage better your particular information technology resources and those resources for which you may be responsible.

In summary, then, to know the 'BIT' means to know the following:

- The computer is inherently a binary machine. That is, no matter what the computer processes, whatever it processes, must ultimately be translated or converted into "binary form".

This is perhaps the most important point to comprehend about the computer and the computer network.

- The binary form means that the electricity flowing through the computer's circuitry is coded using the binary numbering system known to Mathematicians as Base 2.
- The coding into binary form, although done manually by the early computer scientists, has itself been automated over the years. This is possible because of the inherent binary nature of electricity. Electricity is either "ON" or "OFF, and therefore has only 2 possible states. Likewise, the Base 2 numbering system has only 2 digits, "1" and "0". It is a simple matter to represent the 2 states of electricity with the Base 2 numbering system.
- Modern computer and computer network technology has advanced to a point where other techniques are used to translate and transfer BITs in On or Off states, and High or Low pulses. Also, in addition to transferring BITs over Electricity that is BIT encoded electricity, other techniques are used such as light pulse codes (high/low) over fiber-optic cable systems, radio signals for cellular, satellite, microwave signaling and others. However, whatever techniques or technology is deployed to support the transfer, the encoded signals must ultimately translate down to BITs, that is Base 2, binary, on the computer to process, the same, albeit much faster way, it was done on the ENIAC.
- Any number in our highly familiar Base 10 numbering system can be represented in Base 2 and vice-versa. (You may recall Base 10 is what our U.S. currency system is based on....10 pennies = 1 dime, 10 dimes = 1 dollar and so on.). Also important to remember here is that the Base 10 numbering system is based on "positions" or columns such as the 1s, 10s, 100s, 1000s etc. The Base 10 positions form the basis (i.e. positional notation) upon which we can do Base 10-to-Base 2 (binary) and vice-versa translation.
- There is a major distinction between how the computer processes purely mathematical problems and how it processes nonmathematical information. Mathematical calculations take place in "chips" we call "registers". (Chips, like registers, hold and release great quantities of BITs). Nonnmathematical information is largely input and output intensive. As such, text is keyed in, converted to binary for processing, and then stored or processed as output. The binary translation for text occurs on the front-end at input or the backend at output. The characters in text processing are pre-coded via a higher-level coding system and installed on the computer's motherboard. Example: the

ASCII and EBCDIC coding systems. And now we have the 16-BIT UNICODE.

- Textual binary codes are standardized. For example, in EBCDIC, each letter of the alphabet has exactly 8 BITs. Mathematical information, since it is converted directly into binary or Base 2, can have any number of BITs. In our earlier example the number 92 had just 7 BITs. The binary equivalent of the Base 10 number 5 for example would be 1010 or 4 BITs. Also the UNICODE system has been developed and standardized using a '16-BIT' architecture to incorporate ASCII and EBCDIC as well as the character sets for all of the languages of the world
- The BIT is used to measure transmission rates. That de facto standard has evolved to measure the transmission rates of computer networks and other computer network connections. This standard is expressed as bps or BITs-per-second. The more bps, the faster the connection.
- To measure the power of any computer, one needs to know the size of the computer's main Data BUS. The main Data BUS is measured in BITs. Some refer to this as the "width" of the Data BUS. For example, most PCs for the desktop these days are manufactured with a 64-BIT Data BUS. The first PCs used an 8-BIT Data BUS.
- In addition the size and type of the computer's "instruction set" has become an important determinant of the computer's power. This is because at the "BIT-level", conventional computers must scan all instructions (i.e. commands) until it finds the one it needs in order to continue processing the most recent command received on input. The good news is that if the computer is fast enough from its combined Data BUS size and its clock speed, the size of the instruction set may not matter, because the computer is super fast in its scanning anyway. The bad news is that if you are doing applications like rocket science that require every little nanosecond to process you may want to get a reduced instruction set for the computer on which you are going to do rocket science. More good news is that for PCs, MMX technology, which has hit the market in the last year, improves the scanning process even more for certain uses, like multimedia applications and a few other uses. A good example would be desktop publishing where text, graphics, and even video images are all integrated into the same application.
- In addition to size of the main Data BUS, as measured in BIT width (i.e. 64-BIT BUS), the clock speed expressed in Megahertz or MHz and the size and type of instruction set, another power

factor known as MIPS or Millions of Instructions Per Second, has emerged as an important 'Rating Criterion' for assessing the power of a computer. The thing to remember is that it is the combination of BUS size, clock speed, instruction set and a fourth factor known as memory, that delivers the MIPS Rating, not just the instruction set, not just the clock speed or Data BUS.

- And finally, you need to know BIT because it is integral to the BYTE. That's right. You need to know BIT in order to comprehend the BYTE. And the BYTE is Part II of this book. Combined with the fact that we measure network transmission speeds in BITs-per-second and the fact that BYTEs are made up of BITs, you will be able to develop a more comprehensive appreciation for the Y2K set of problems by solidifying your understanding of the BIT. You can relate BIT to all Y2K component problems including: embedded system chips, general hardware, as well as software and the main options being used today to perform Y2K remediation. But a good understanding of the BIT is integral to fully understanding the BYTE. Although the BYTE is Part II of the book, it is the other half of knowing computer technology, including Y2K, for now and beyond the year 2000. The BYTE is the foundation for several other higher level aspects of the computer, much the same way that the BIT is the foundation for those aspects of the computer and computer network which are at the machine level.

PART II:

The BYTE?

6

Why Do I Need to Know the BYTE?

In Part I, I discussed the BIT. The BIT is simple, yet complicated all at the same time, depending on your perspective. People who have studied and worked at the BIT level (i.e. programmers, computer and network engineers) in general, are able to understand readily the BIT definitions offered in Part I. If you are new to the computer or have never worked at the BIT level, most likely you need to study the BIT definitions offered here to gain this understanding. The BIT, believe it or not, is more clearly definable than the BYTE. Yet both BIT and BYTE remain largely confused concepts in our world of computers and of computer networking.

The fact that clear definitions of the BIT are not well established in society at large, even after 50 years of computer automation, is a function (or dysfunction, if you will) of how our society defines new concepts, particularly those which are technical. Until and unless a concept is embraced by our culture, it will remain locked up forever in the throngs of technical dictionaries and classroom textbooks. Given this presupposition, where do we go with defining the BYTE?

The BYTE leads us upward through the computer and on out to the higher levels of computer networking. To be sure, this is where we humans derive value and meaning from the underlying supportive technology of the computer, which is inherently binary and driven by the BIT.

You need to know the BYTE because the BYTE is where we find meaning in all that the computer network can process. The BYTE is what the machine-level BITs are translated into. That is, machine language at the BIT level of the computer or computer network becomes meaningful information through the formation of BYTEs. For example, the letter 'A' has a pre-coded set of BITs at the machine level.

I would like to start off with the distinction that I introduced in Part I. There are 2 types of BYTEs relative to computer network processing. These 2 types of BYTEs are mathematical and nonmathematical. You need to understand both types of BYTEs, not only to grasp the differences between them, but also to recognize how the computer and computer network processes, displays, prints and stores meaningful information.

With respect to the Y2K problem, hardware needs to be designed at manufacture to accept a 4-BYTE year field. And the calendar year field can and should be capable of being manipulated through the software to be either a nonmathematical or mathematical BYTE depending on the user's needs.

In other words, this comes down to the difference between processing a calendar year that may be used mathematically for calculating something like principal and interest on a loan with a term going into the year 2000 and beyond, and the processing of a calendar year 2000 or beyond that may be embedded in a word-processing document (i.e.nonmathematical). Both require 4-BYTE year fields, but one is mathematical, one is nonmathematical. You may be surprised, but hardware not capable of processing a 4-BYTE year could handle a nonmathematical year of 2000 and beyond. This is because it is embedded in a word-processing document. Here the computer hardware treats it like it treats any other textual information.

For over 50 years, computers have been processing calendar dates using only the last two digits of the year (e.g. 1998 uses 98). This will not work for mathematical BYTEs when our calendar reaches the year 2000. The computer won't calculate correctly with a year of 00. Many issues which are at the core of things like the Y2K problem have concurrent implications for computer storage management, application software, network transmission, and other problem areas.

Mathematical BYTEs are what the computer generates in support of calculations. The computer uses directly the binary numbering system to process all mathematical calculations. Thus, depending on the size and type of calculation being processed, BYTE storage requirements for mathematical numbers or mathematical results are considered variable. That is, the computer on any given day may process one or more calculations which do not exceed, say 4 digits. Say you are using the computer to balance your checkbook. Typically, we do not exceed $1,000 in any of our check transactions. Compare this to using the computer to process checks you may have to write at work to pay your company's suppliers. In this company example, it is typical for checks to always be over $10,000. The BYTE processing and storage requirements of these two mathematical transactions will be different or variable.

This differs from requirements for nonmathematical BYTEs. Nonmathematical BYTEs are predefined based on a standardized binary coding system. In Part I, I referred to, for example, several character coding systems including, the ASCII, EBCDIC and UNICODE standardized character coding systems. These precoded standardized systems assign a certain binary code to represent each and every element in the coding system. Because it is pre-coded and standardized, letters, numbers and special characters of the nonmathematical ilk are always going to have the same BYTE storage requirements. And this BYTE size storage requirement will be based on whatever standardized binary coding character set is running on the computer. For instance, with UNICODE, each and every nonmathematical BYTE will always process, print out, display and store, using 16 BITs, because UNICODE is a 16-BIT binary coding system.

A simple way to distinguish mathematical from nonmathematical BYTEs, which use numbers, is to consider the use of a date such as 03/07/98. In a word-processing software package, let us say that you entered this as the date in a memo you were completing. Will the computer process it as a date? The meaning at the higher level, that is, human level, would be March 7, 1998. Or, will the computer process it as a mathematical calculation? That is, 03 divided by 07 divided by 98. Mathematically the result would be .0043731.

The answer once again is that in the word-processor it would be processed non-mathematically as a date requiring 8 BYTEs, 6 nonmathematical numbers and 2 special characters-the slashes. Therefore, nonmathematical BYTEs are fixed. Each character is always 1 BYTE. And each nonmathematical character will always have a preset number of BITs which is predetermined by the specific standardized character coding system installed on the computer at the time of manufacturing. The preinstalled character coding system cannot be changed on the computer. It comes with the computer upon purchase and stays with it for the computer's lifetime.

If we enter the same thing on a mathematical spreadsheet, the 2 slashes would be interpreted by the computer as commands to divide. The 6 numbers would be stored temporarily as 3 BYTEs, each BYTE containing 03, 07, 98 respectively. As such, we would get a result of .0043731. And this result would be stored in 1-single BYTE. Thus, Mathematical BYTEs have a variable nature depending on the numbers and sizes of the numbers involved in the calculation.

You can see that the computer does distinguish numbers as nonmathematical and mathematical. This distinction is necessary because the computer and the computer network are inherently binary. The computer evolved initially as a machine that could only do mathematical calculations in binary. By building on the binary nature of the computer, we were able to add on the nonmathematical coding systems, albeit still binary coding systems. But "fixed" binary coding systems, in order to enable the strictly binary computer to do other nonmathematical applications such as textual processing, e-mail, word-processing etc.

You may ask, "so what"? The computer software takes care of it. Why do I need to bother to understand this nonmathematical versus mathematical difference? Well, okay. There is more reasoning to it.

It is not just in the processing of BYTEs, but also in the storage of BYTEs. The type of computer storage used in nonmathematical is the same as the storage for mathematical. But the mathematical processing uses, in addition, the Arithmetic Logic Unit or ALU. And since mathematical BYTEs have a variable size, they may require more storage to contain them during processing. Whereas nonmathematical BYTEs always require the same pre-coded amount of storage space.

These BYTE differences are important for you to know because it will enable you to distinguish a powerful computer from one, which may not be so powerful. And in the case of Y2K issues, you need to understand the importance of getting a Y2K compliant computer system if and when you should buy. Y2K compliance means that your computer can process a 4-BYTE calendar date field, whether this date field is processing non-mathematical or mathematical BYTEs.

If you already have an older computer and all you will ever do is word-processing than you can continue to use this computer beyond Y2K. Because your word-processor will treat the date as a non-mathematical BYTE field. You may have to reset your system date to some year prior to Y2K depending specifically on your hardware type, but you would not need to purchase a new system. Also you would not get the current date from the hardware system itself. But if all you ever do is word-processing you would not need to be concerned. You could simply key in the correct date in your document. Check with your hardware supplier for your specific hardware type and how to deal with the system date.

BYTEs of either type are stored temporarily in memory. One BYTE of either ilk takes up one unit of main memory storage. Some refer to it as BYTE unit storage. A character, nonmathematical BYTE, will always take up one BYTE of memory. One character, one BYTE unit of memory. On the other hand, mathematical BYTEs take up one or more BYTEs (units) of memory, depending on the size of the number(s) to be stored. Main memory, or simply 'memory', is measured in total BYTEs.

Memory is one of the major power factors of any computer. The more memory you have onboard, the more you can do, and the faster you can do it. But as we get into these higher level meanings for the BYTE, it becomes easy to forget that the BYTE has its beginnings in 'so many BITs'. So, remember-all BYTEs have BIT beginnings.

In addition, we need to remember that BYTE-size units of storage in memory do not just exist without any order. There is a rationale for organizing the huge numbers of BYTEs that get stored, albeit temporarily, in memory. And that would be that each BYTE-size unit of main memory storage is addressable. That's right. The computer, under directions from the operating system stores BYTEs in memory, based on address.

The units of memory storage exist in a particular sequence. Beginning with the first BYTE unit location all the way up to the 16MB, 32MB, 64MB unit location, depending on how much main memory capacity you have loaded on your computer. You could say that this addressing scheme is hardware based, because it is based on the memory chips. Their physical installation position on the motherboard determines the order , sequence, and address at which BYTEs will be stored.

Simply put, main memory is a string or sequence of units of storage. The power, or the magic if you will, comes in when you consider: the computer can store BYTEs in these chips at nearly the speed of light, remember the order or sequence in which it did the storing, determine an address location for each and every BYTE unit of memory storage, and retrieve any and all BYTE units currently stored in memory.

We have distinguished BYTEs as being mathematical or nonmathematical. And now, we have established that so many BITs make up a BYTE. Mathematical BYTEs can vary in size. However, nonmathematical BYTEs are predefined in terms of how many BITs per BYTE, based on the standardized character code, being used on any particular computer. Each type of BYTE will have varying memory and storage requirements. Mathematical BYTE unit memory and BYTE storage requirements vary according to the size and type of calculations being processed. BYTEs which equal a letter, a nonmathematical number, or a special character, have predefined BYTE unit memory and BYTE storage requirements.

One salient feature of all BYTEs is to recognize that we human users of the computer and the computer network derive meaning or subjective value from the computer's output through the great numbers of BYTEs which get displayed for us across the screen, printed for us on hardcopy output and which are stored permanently for us on secondary storage. It helps facilitate better comprehension of the BYTE if we know its underlying origins.

Knowing the BYTE aids greatly in your comprehension of both primary and secondary storage. Knowing the BYTE means knowing that what you are currently processing is concurrently stored in BYTE form in main memory. And knowing that what is stored takes up BYTE unit storage capacity in memory. In addition, when you store or save what you are working on in secondary storage (i.e. disk) it takes up physical residence in BYTE form on your disk or diskette.

Knowing the BYTE means you are able to manage your storage requirements; both primary and secondary. It means you know your BYTE limitations in terms of how and what you can process. If you are working on a document that is 80 pages long, is it better to store 79 of the pages on secondary and continue your work on the 80th page from active main memory? Or, is it better to load the entire document in main memory and continue working on page 80. If you leave 79 pages in permanent storage and only work on the current page, namely page 80 in main memory, you are using much less main memory and therefore, your work will process much faster.

When you are done with the work progressing onward from page 80, you can then call up the separate document containing the other 79 pages. Then it simply means inserting at the end of page 79 all the work you have done on the new separate document progressing onward from page 80. Save the revised document which is now presumably 80+ pages long. It now becomes the new "master", if you will.

Save the document resulting from work beginning at page 80 as a new document. Next session, begin work on this new document, and you may delete everything in it, except for the last page. And then simply repeat the process described above to insert the most current material into the 'master' document. In this way you are optimizing both primary and secondary storage.

Given the above suppositions on the BYTE, it becomes obvious why we need to know the BYTE. Working from the higher level downward to the machine level, that is, the level where everything on the computer and or the computer network is in BITs, our first stop is in the area of storage.

We need to know the BYTE because secondary storage, whether it be diskette, hard disk, CD-ROM or Writable CD is measured in-you guessed it-BYTEs. A 3.5" diskette, for instance, stores 1.44MBs. Hard disk capacities are all now coming out, except for the smallest of computers, with multi-giga BYTE capacities. CD technology now at the leading edge is coming in with capacities beyond 500MBs. Imagine 1 single CD having the capacity of at least 372 each 3.5" diskettes. Also, just this year, we now have the 'SuperDiskette'. It is a 3.5" diskette, which can hold up to 180MB, or the equivalent of 120 of the now, if I may say, older diskettes. Do you think an appreciation for the BYTE is relevant here?

With secondary storage, knowing the BYTE is essential because of the tremendous storage capacity that any computer network user now has. I sometimes fantasize about what the world would be like if everyone had as many dollars in the bank. What kind of socio-economic climate would we have? Would folks be trading exuberantly on the stock market, buying and selling property, suing each other, etc.? Intuitively, I want to say that we as a society would end up in chaos. And it would occur at roughly the speed of light.

Fortunately, this capacity to which I refer, is limited to the computer user's secondary BYTE storage and not savings expressed in dollars. But by extension, we can surmise potentialities that may develop if society were to relegate more and more dependence on information stored in secondary storage. When you can replicate (i.e. duplicate or copy) billions of BYTEs of information in less than a second of time, you have a certain power which can be used for the good, and which can be used for the bad. Knowing the BYTE is the first step to comprehending this paradox.

How you then use the BYTE(s) in storage becomes more operational-managerial in many respects. Certainly you need to know BYTE to know how big your files are, how long and how much it will cost to transfer your files. Also, how much secondary storage you would need to install a given software package and then to operate that package. Software packages are groups of one or more files. Files are measured in BYTEs. Files require BYTE storage capacity to take up residence on your hard disk. And, if you backup your secondary storage, you need to know BYTE again to know the types of capacities you will need to support your backup.

At the higher levels, BYTEs are what convey meaning to us users.

A letter, nonmathematical as well as mathematical numbers, or a special character, is one of the higher level definitions of a BYTE. These letters, numbers and other characters are displayed on the monitor screen, reside in memory while you are using the computer, can be printed in hardcopy format and can be transferred via a computer network to some remote location.

Being able to convey meaning, replicate, store, output, and transfer meaningful BYTE information, is a power, which every computer user has. If you do not know the BYTE, you cannot comprehend this power, or the chaos, which will ensue from inappropriate management of it.

Moreover, primary storage plays a critical role in the use and management of the computer. Primary storage has 2 components: Read Only Memory (ROM) and Random Access Memory (RAM).

ROM on any computer is a given. It is set at the factory. Perhaps its most important function is that it contains the computer's initial program load or IPL for short. Every time you turn on the computer, the IPL gets loaded from ROM, into active memory, which is RAM.

Today RAM is also referred to as main memory, or simply, memory. The more you have, the more power your computer has. Memory is measured in BYTEs.

Your computer's IPL will take up the same amount of BYTE storage in memory each and every time you turn the computer on. BYTE requirements for your ROM are a constant. However, it is useful to understand that the IPL from ROM gets loaded in units of BYTE storage into the beginning addressable units of storage that make up your computer's active memory.

From the IPL the computer loads the operating system (OS) software which is pre-installed onto your computer's hard disk. The OS takes up residence in addressable memory in the next sequentially available units of memory storage. That is, immediately following the IPL. Again in BYTE unit form, just like the IPL.

The IPL and OS load into memory upon turning on the electrical power and activates the computer. Activation brings the computer system to a point where the typical user can begin work. We refer to this point these days as the 'Start' position or coming to the START button. This is the start position on any computer running the WINDOWS 95 or now the WINDOWS 98 Operating System. On computers controlled by other OSs the computer will have a different start position. But the point is that the computer has to load some software, the IPL and the OS first in order to activate the computer and get the computer to a point where the user can run applications.

At the Start position, the user can click on the icons, which represent the word-processor, e-mail, WEB Search, or whatever applications are being supported on their particular computer. (Icons are pictorial buttons on your screen that represent individual applications. For instance, with e-mail, there may be an icon that looks like a little mailbox.) Each and every subsequent program or application that the user may run will be loaded into memory in BYTE unit form in the next sequentially available units of main memory.

Lastly, any data or information files, (files are like larger containers for BYTEs) are also loaded in BYTE unit form into memory as these files are created, opened or downloaded. These files take up residence in the sequentially next available storage locations in memory.

Therefore you can see that much is loaded into memory. Active memory! What is loaded in primary memory supports the computer user's current session on the computer. Primary memory is measured in BYTEs. And it remains active for the session until the point when the user closes out the application(s) and/or turns off the power to the computer.

You need to know the BYTE because primary storage, memory, is measured and managed in BYTEs. BYTEs take up residence for the life of the current computer session in addressable units of storage. It is useful to consider that a single BYTE of information: a letter, number or a special character, will require exactly one unit of storage in memory to be active.

Thinking about the BYTE in terms of being a single character of information helps to understand how many BYTEs are typically needed to create or open a meaningful file of BYTEs, or to set off a software package which is made up of one or more files of BYTEs. Since everything has to be loaded into memory to become usable, the road to meaningful information being displayed on your monitor, output to your printer, or transferred over your computer network, is through BYTE unit addressable memory (i.e. primary storage). If the information you seek cannot be loaded in BYTE form into your computer's memory, you will not be able to get what you seek. Knowing the BYTE means knowing this important element.

To summarize why we need to know the BYTE, it is the major element necessary for us users to understand how it is possible for the computer to process and deliver meaningful information, on the monitor display, over the network and through hard copy printed output.

You need to know the BYTE to comprehend how information is processed through memory. The more capacity for storing BYTEs in memory, the more power your computer will have in terms of how much it can process at any given time, and how fast it can process. Knowing the BYTE means you can manage and measure your memory capacity.

You need to know BYTE to understand how information is processed, saved and retreived from secondary storage. In particular, hard disk, diskette, CD-ROM and the forthcoming writable CDs.

Like memory, management and measurement of BYTE capacities, become important computer user tasks. Knowing the BYTE means you can save and retrieve BYTE filled files of information on selected secondary storage devices, such as the hard disk, and that you can selectively choose at the time of saving or retrieval which secondary storage device to utilize among those that you have connected to your computer's main Data BUS.

Lastly, you need to know the BYTE, in order to know how the BYTE is organized with other BYTEs to organize into larger BYTE containers known as Files of BYTEs, or simply files. The computer and the computer network both are "File-driven". (This is to say that they are 'BYTE-driven', which is to say that files are 'BIT-driven' as well.)

On the computer, so many BITs, make up a mathematical and or a nonmathematical BYTE. So many BYTEs, make up a file. You will truly have arrived with the BYTE, and will be at one with the computer and computer network when you can comprehend from the BYTE-perspective how files are created, stored, printed, retrieved, modified, and when necessary, deleted.

7

The BYTE Definitions?

In Part I we talked about the BIT as being coded electricity, which operates at the 'machine level'. In the mathematical sense of computer processing, everything must ultimately translate down to the 'machine level'. That is, it must convert to the coded electrical form in order to be processed. Since the computer is inherently 'binary', no higher-level or pre-coded numbering systems are required to process mathematical applications.

We also talked about several pre-coded "character sets" which operate at a higher level than pure, binary BITs used in mathematical applications. For the computer to process the letter 'A', the computer's pre-coded character set must translate the letter 'A' into a binary equivalent form prior to processing. The computer's circuitry incorporates additional 'circuit traces' or 'paths' on the motherboard to accommodate character processing. Also, the computer has hardwired into its processor box a specific unique, pre-coded character set to do this translation.

All computers do not have the same character set manufactured into them. This has been a major source of 'incompatibility' among computers. But this has changed dramatically over the last several years. There is a drive worldwide to make computers fully compatible regardless of what company does the manufacturing. This is referred to as 'Open Systems' architecture. Other synonymous terms are 'Interoperable' and 'Portable'.

The continuing evolution of the computer, therefore, will include more 'open' and 'interoperable' technologies. The UNICODE pre-coded character set is a good example of this. We discussed the evolution of pre-coded character sets in Part I. As you now know, there have been several pre-coded character sets over the years, starting with the 5-BIT Baudot Code, BCD, EBCDIC, ASCII, and lastly the UNICODE.

UNICODE reflects well the tremendous benefits that can be attained through fully compatible computers for all of society. At the same time, it highlights in my mind the ghastly social trends that could develop if incompatible systems with disparate onboard coding schemes from the manufacturer are permitted to flourish. On the one hand, it is visible how 'compatible' systems will benefit society because computer uses, and therefore dependency on them, is growing. On the other hand, if incompatible systems flourish, there are several social and economic factors that could evolve with this incompatibility. (i.e. time-consuming miscommunications, which now could occur at nearly the speed of light. Imagine mass, miscommunications at the speed of light. We essentially would be automating chaos.) What constitutes a BYTE on a computer is at the core of this 'compatibility/incompatibility' issue.

As such, it is not a suprise that the BYTE is at the core of the Y2K set of problems.

Therefore, moving forward, as we turn from the BIT to the BYTE, higher-level issues now will begin to surface relative to the computer and computer network. We said earlier that computer 'applications' basically are some use of the computer. These include word-processing, e-mail, etc. The BYTE becomes an essential element in using, understanding, and managing the computer. This is because in order for a computer to be used effectively, memory and storage must be taken into account and weighed in all applications you may desire to install and use on your computer, any computer and any computer network. The BYTE is the major factor in measuring memory and storage.

Like BIT, however, the term BYTE has gone through some evolution. The etymology of the BYTE is unclear at this time. A good understanding of the evolution of the computer pinpoints the BYTE's inception to be approximately the time that the early computer pioneers began to invent and implement techniques for achieving 'active memory' and the storage of BITs, both dynamic and static types of storage respectively. These two specialized types of storage have evolved in many circles and in textbooks. They are called primary storage and secondary Storage respectively. To the lay person today, primary is referred to as 'memory' and secondary is known simply as 'disk'. Sometimes called hard disk or diskette, but more often than not just 'disk'. Many students will incorrectly refer to it as the 'hard drive'. But in reality, the hard drive is the thing which contains the actual 'hard disk', where the BYTEs are stored.

Generally speaking, in my experience, I've found the BYTE and related essentials to be easier for folks at all levels to understand than the BIT. I think this is because with the BYTE we are moving toward the higher-level aspects of the computer. As such more uses of the computer can be associated with the BYTE to which more people can relate.

If we take all of the computer dictionaries available today and assemble all of the popular definitions on BYTE, we would end up with, for the most part, seven definitions. Like the BIT, I have found that there is much confusion with the BYTE. And, indeed, much of what is contained in Part II follows our understanding of the BIT and the confusion out there about the BYTE.

Popular Definitions of the Byte

A BYTE is:

1) Smallest unit of Information on a computer.

2) Smallest unit of storage on a computer.

3) A deprecated term for a single unit of storage on a computer.

4) One or more BITs which taken together form a single 'addressable' unit on a computer.

5) How the computer represents a single character on output.

6) A pre-coded set of 8 BITs translated by the Computer

7) 8 BITs

If we take number 1 we run into the dilemma with defining BIT. That is, it can be the smallest unit of information. But information implies subjective meaning for everyone. Frankly, computers are incapable of subjective meaning. Computers can be programmed to make decisions that ostensibly portray things like emotions and subjectivity. A programmer has to pre-code this, however, into the computer's software. And information can be anything from soup to nuts.

Number 2, the "smallest unit of storage on a computer" above, presents a dilemma of being the smallest unit and of being a unit of storage. All BYTEs, we will discuss, become 'Units of Storage' at least once during processing on a computer. Therefore, when I clarify number 1 definition above, you will be able to see how the number 2 above can be an accurate definition.

The third definition, "a single unit of storage", is accurate. A BYTE is, as we will see, a single unit of storage. But much is left unsaid here. This definition would be highly meaningful to the computer scientist and computer engineers. But most computer users do not have this type of background. Also there are two distinct types of storage on a computer which have similarities and differences in how they process BYTEs. We will be discussing these differences over the next few chapters.

The number 4 definition specifies that a BYTE can be at least one

BIT as well as multiple BITs. And, specifies further that there is an 'addressable unit' or 'grouping' of BITs which make up the BYTE. Addressing is a key element of computer storage. This definition is highly accurate because it specifies from the 'machine level' what constitutes the BYTE. And again it is a more technical definition. My guess is that if you asked a computer scientist, "what is a BYTE?", you would get a definition like number 4.

Number 5, "how the computer represents a character on output" is partially correct. But, again, much is left unsaid. BYTEs are more than just characters. What if we need to output the results of a mathematical calculation? This definition therefore does add to the confusion. And it is limited in what it defines about the BYTE. Again, much is left unsaid. Managing your computer's BYTE capacity requires knowing how the computer stores the BYTE, in addition to representing the BYTE on the screen or in a hard-copy output. (Hardcopy is printed or paper output.)

The sixth definition is not contradictable from a non-mathematical perspective. In this definition, a BYTE equals any character defined by a pre-coded set of BITs which are defined by the computer's standardized 'character set'. You will recall from Part I our discussion of the numerous standardized characters coding systems that are installed on computers. ASCII, EBCDIC and now UNICODE. Each standardized coding set uses a different number of BITs to formulate a non-mathematical BYTE, like the letter 'A', for instance.

The shortcomings with the sixth definition are that it does not respond to the mathematical side of the computer house and its does not acknowledge the BYTE's requirement for storage, that is to be stored somewhere, if only temporarily. If we cannot store the BYTE we cannot process the BYTE. That is, upon input, during internal processing and upon output. Storage and the BYTE go hand-in-hand. Understanding storage, you will see, becomes the challenge with understanding the BYTE.

Also important to understand in the sixth BYTE definition is that numbers defined in these character sets are not necessarily 'calculation-based'. For example if you are creating a word-processing document such as a formal letter, you key in somewhere at the top of the document the "date". To do this you use, perhaps, numbers and slashes, 01/28/98. The numbers in this date are not the same as the numbers used, say, to ADD 2+8. One is character-based, the other is mathematical. This is an important distinction with the Y2K set of problem(s) looming just ahead.

Last, but not least, number 7 is the definition which is the uninformed choice of many non-science majors, the general public, and those who have come to the conclusion that they don't need to know anything technical about the computer. This is unfortunate. At least equally unfortunate is the fact that we have not done enough to clarify those important aspects of the computer, which are necessary for responsible computer usage.

Number 7 is an oversimplification any way you toss it. It fails to consider any of the related important elements such as storage. It also fails to consider 16-BIT encoding. In our description of UNICODE, in Part I, we covered how this standardized character coding set used a 16-BIT code. As such, a UNICODE BYTE would require 16 BITs to process. However, depending on your perspective and what coding system the computer in question is using, it could be viewed merely as a simple definition of the BYTE. The EBCDIC code uses eight BITs per nonmathematical BYTE.

Within the subsequent pages, I will clarify and embellish the above definitions. To accomplish this I will take the major BYTE-related components which are located inside and out of the processor box, which in one way or another, processes BYTEs, beginning with where we left off with the BIT in Part I. It is clear that several factors need to be evaluated in formulating a comprehensive definition of BYTE.

The above definitions demand some clarification for such factors: storage, unit size, addressing, and character versus mathematical, representation and what constitutes information. And I will provide this in the following chapters.

For now, to continue on our BYTE journey (as it is surely not a destination), I offer you my definition of a BYTE.

One or more consecutive BIT(s) which taken as a complete unit of binary encoded BIT(s) formulate either a mathematical number, a nonmathematical character (or set of nonmathematical special characters). A BYTE must take up temporary residence as a single addressable unit in active computer memory in order for the computer to display, store, print or otherwise process it as meaningful information. A BYTE typically becomes one of many other related BYTEs contained in larger units of storage known as files. At the networking level, one or more BYTEs are translated and encapsulated into larger units of dynamic storage known as BIT streams, packets, frames, blocks, or envelopes for the purpose of supporting network transmission. The BYTE has emerged as the single most important metric for measuring computer memory, storage and along with BIT overhead on networks, the overall bandwidth and throughput of meaningful information. Mathematical BYTEs vary in BIT size according to how large of a number needs to be calculated or otherwise processed. Nonmathematical BYTEs defined through ASCII, EBCDIC or UNICODE will be 7-BIT, 8-BIT or 16-BIT size, respectively, depending on which standard coding system is in use.

The Mathematical BYTE

The whole evolution of the BYTE is truly what brings meaningful information to the entire universe of computers and computer network technology. The BYTE is what enables the inherent language of the computer to be translated into natural languages among numerous and varied applications. For the most part here I'm referring to 'non-mathematical' applications.

Though even in mathematical applications today there are many integrated 'textu. l and graphical' uses. Spreadsheet applications are a perfect example of this. Spreadsheet applications calculate. Spreadsheets are used in thousands of different ways to support financial decisions, and other calculation-based functions. At the same time, the spreadsheet software incorporates features to permit textual processing in the form of column headers, date(s), and a whole range of 'non-mathematical' formatting options.

In Part I we discussed 'binary' as being the only true language of computers, in the very first computer as well as in modern day computers. We also discussed how the computer processed the 'non-mathematical' using binary pre-coded, standardized character sets. These two 'paths' if you will, mathematical and nonmathematical, on the computer are still, today, essentially the same. Now it's time for those of us who use the computer for mostly "non-mathematical" applications to see how the BYTE plays a part in converting the 'binary' into meaningful information for both mathematical and non-mathematical applications.

Mathematical meaning is derived through 'binary' translation. Other numbering systems are used to make the process more efficient. In addition to the required binary we have: Base 16 or "Hexadecimal"(Hex), Base 8 or "Octal" and our very own Base 10, which mathematicians refer to as "DECIMAL". This is where BYTE definition numbers 1 through 4 come into play.

A binary mathematical number, translated by decimal so that it can be rendered in a manner that we humans readily understand on the monitor screen or in hard copy, may be equal to a single BYTE. A solid single BYTE. Observe that I say, and would like to emphasize "may" be equal to a single BYTE. It may also require, depending on the size of the binary number, more than a single BYTE to process and store on the computer. Larger numbers require more than one BYTE of storage, for example, to store in main memory or to calculate by adding to another larger number. The larger the number(s) used the more storage cells will be required: to translate the number to its binary equivalent, to store the translated BITs in memory for processing, to calculate a result if it is used in a calculation, and then possibly, to store the result of the calculation.

The Binary numeric is strictly "ON" or "OFF" electrical states or BIT(s) coded by us humans with "1s" and "0s" as we discussed in Part I. That is to say by the software we use. We actually never see the binary translation going on behind the scenes. And it happens magically at nearly the speed of light. Each and every mathematical BYTE has a corresponding coded set of BIT(s) formulated automatically through the Base 2 or binary numbering system during processing.

The challenge now becomes understanding the storage component here. We refer to this today as memory. For Mathematical applications, registers from the ALU or arithmetic logic unit work in tandem with the chips that make up the computer's memory. Now, here is the 64 million dollar question, "how does main memory store numbers to be used in calculations?" The answer is, in single, addressable units—called BYTEs.

The more single, addressable units of storage on your computer, the more powerful your computer will be because it can 'store' more, individual numbers used in mathematical calculations. These 'memory-storage' units are sometimes referred to as memory 'cells'. These storage units can be a variable in terms of the size of the binary equivalent number they can hold. The size of the BYTE that a memory cell can hold can be manipulated through the software to a certain extent. Other numbering systems (i.e. octal, hex) can play a part in optimizing the size of memory units. However, these are functions that programmer types might do, not something for the non-mathematical user.

Therefore, any number that is purely mathematical , takes up storage in more than one storage location on the computer for the time it takes the computer to complete processing. These locations are in the ALU and in main memory. The binary equivalent number 'stored' in one or more units of addressable memory constitutes one or more BYTEs in the mathematical sense. The binary numbers stored in the ALU are not directly addressable and are numbers stored only for the length of the calculation.

The Non-mathematical BYTE

Most folks using the computer do not really care about the mathematical sense of it all. They want to use the computer, that is, run their specific applications. Binary problems, if and when they occur, can be turned over to the guy who sold them the computer. Or, they can call the number on the maintenance contract, or call the department in the company that supports computers, etc..

And occasionally problems occur. Your computer can get locked up. The wrong keys may be pressed causing a failure in storage or in processing. Sometimes you will see a strange error message on the screen. Usually these messages are in text form and display 'garbage' characters on the screen. Much of the time when this happens, the computer is trying to translate signals at the binary level for which there is no pre-coded character set, or binary equivalent. Usually the numbers in the screen message reflect the storage addresses in main memory that are involved in the error. I point it out because it is interesting. Moreover, it is a decent insertion point for explaining BYTEs from the non-mathematical perspective.

When we discussed the definitions of the BYTE, you got a good summary of the prevailing fragments of information which in part describe the BYTE. One of the major points brought out is that there is an important distinction between mathematical and nonmathematical BYTEs. Further, we explained that the size of the mathematical BYTE in terms of the BITs which must be stored in main memory is a variable BIT size which is contingent upon the size of the number being processed. The number 6 million would take more BITs than the number '6' to represent in binary form, for example.

With non-mathematical the BYTE is not of a variable size. It is the size which is pre-coded in the computer's on board standardized character set. Most PCs and Notebooks today come with either ASCII or the leading edge character set known as UNICODE. (With UNICODE the computer requires 16 BITs to process a nonmathematical BYTE.)

The 5-BIT Baudot code was never designed to be used by computers, even though it played a major part in providing the basis for development of the 6-BIT BCD code which indeed was the first standard character set used by computers. BCD is no longer used today. The original 7-BIT ASCII code is very popular . The EBCDIC code is still widely used on the IBM mainframe class of computers. And lastly, the UNICODE is being deployed on new PCs and individual computers as well as shared computers. Since it subsumes both ASCII and EBCDIC, it is fully compatible with the prevailing standard character sets, namely ASCII and EBCDIC. UNICODE is becoming the standard character set for today and the future.

As such, we can update our definition of the BYTE. One through four on our list still hold for the non-mathematical. All we need do is to integrate them into one. That is, a 'BYTE is a single, addressable, unit of storage'. To this we now add definitions 5 and update 6 and 7. Taking number 5, we need a pre-coded set of BITs for each single character that can possibly be used in processing, printing and or displaying a character. Number5 duly responds to this need. Number 6 responds to the need for the BYTE to be "pre-coded and standardized". Seven, though, needs to be updated because computers now incorporate 16-BIT encoding for character sets. So it can be either 7, 8 or 16-BIT, not just 8-BIT.

Like the mathematical processing of binary numbers, non-mathematical characters get processed in the binary sense. However, character BYTEs are input and output only. Character BYTEs, like mathematical BYTEs do get stored in memory for the duration of whatever processing is taking place. Unlike the mathematical, however, non-mathematical character BYTEs do not get 'stored' temporarily in the computer's ALU section.

Just like binary numbers, each and every character has a BIT code, except that with character BYTEs the code is pre-determined by the computer's standard character set (i.e. ASCII, EBCDIC, UNICODE). Character BYTEs do not result from a numerical calculation. Mathematical numbers on the computer become binary numbers, pure coded electricity. No standardized character coding system is needed for mathematical numbers to be converted to binary.

8

The BYTE and Storage

Primary storage is dynamic, active and volatile. It is the type of storage that is temporary, but not quite as temporary as storage used, for example, in the ALU section of the CPU to process mathematical calculations. Primary storage is made up of memory (Random Access Memory) chips and ROM or 'Read-Only-Memory'. Memory must work in tandem with the ALU for completing calculations. I will also clarify ROM's function.

Many people confuse memory with storage. It is useful to consider memory as a sort of dynamic storage. When you are done and you close your files and turn the computer off, memory becomes all zeroed out. That is, empty chips, all sequentially organized onto the motherboard with absolutely no BITs stored whatsoever.

Without electrical power, memory is essentially all 'off' state. Because of this important characteristic we refer to memory as being 'volatile'. That is, if the power is turned off or goes off for any reason, memory is wiped out.

We said that memory is made up of storage chips. Comparing memory chips to those chips used in the ALU, we can say that they are similar in their manufacturing make-up. A chip is a chip is a chip. Now there are differences in function to be noted. But essentially we are talking about, you guessed it—chips. However, they operate to support storage in two distinct ways. ALU chips are called 'registers' and are calculation-oriented. If there is no calculation on input, then the ALU is not needed by the computer. Whereas the chips in memory are used each and every time the computer is 'booted' up (turned on) and with every single transaction, including calculations and all other application types.

Storage registers in the ALU are more dynamic and used specifically for the calculation being processed at the moment in the computer, however simple or complex the calculation may be. (Now, it is perhaps important to recognize that a moment inside the computer is a moment like no other. I'm referring to the magical fact that 'moments' inside the computer are measured at nearly the speed of light.)

The numbers used in calculations, as well as the numeric results from such calculations, for example, are also 'stored' in memory. Once in memory irrespective of whether or not the numbers are mathematical or character-based, these values are accessible for display on the monitor screen, output to the printer or to be saved on your hard disk. So you can see that in order to get anything useful out of the computer, it must first get stored even though temporarily in memory. Therefore, memory is an important power determinant of the computer.

Primary storage that includes both ROM and memory resets to complete "off state" each and every time the power to the computer is cut off. This is why many application manuals recommend to you in using these applications that you take steps to SAVE or "Backup...by SAVING" your work as you complete it, rather than, when you complete your current session on the computer. You never know when you might lose power.

If you are working on a substantial document and have not yet saved it, and there is a loss in power, you would lose your document. (All BYTEs would be wiped out, just as if you turned a light bulb switch off.) Also, it is recommended that you SAVE your work before you request the computer to print it. This is because your computer can potentially "lock up" when sending your work to print, and if you have to restart the computer you would shut down the contents of memory. Consequently you would lose whatever information you had actively stored in memory.

Memory is active, fast and available to the user for application(s) processing for the duration of the current session provided that the computer has sufficient electrical power. Now modern computers can use normal house current or in the case of many PC notebooks, and the newer, yet, smaller palm-top PCs, all come with additional battery units so they can be used on the go. However, if power is lost to the computer, memory-type storage is wiped out. Primary storage which includes both ROM and memory requires electrical power to come to active life and to stay active. And the computer will come to life each and every time the computer is turned on. But if the computer loses power during processing, any BYTE form information that had been stored, even though temporarily, in memory, is completely wiped out.

Memory has emerged over the years as one of the most important factors in determining the power of a computer. Along with 'BIT-size of the main data BUS, the clock speed (MHz) and the size and type of instruction set; memory storage enables users to actively store multiple applications at the same time and work concurrently with multiple applications. (For an example of concurrent you could have memory active with a word-processor, spreadsheet, database and e-mail. All at the same moment.) In addition, the more memory storage, the faster the computer will run because it can 'store' upfront the programs and data it needs to operate, versus having to fetch the programs and data that may be stored on secondary storage each time these things are needed in the current user session.(secondary storage means your CD, hard disk) We will talk more about secondary storage in the next chapter.

Read Only Memory (ROM)

Now to be fair and accurate in my description, I must clarify more precisely primary storage. Primary storage is actually made up of two major components. One, as discussed, is called memory that is that part of primary that is volatile, active and dynamic. The more memory you have in your computer, the faster your computer will be. Also the more applications you can run concurrently. Memory is measured in BYTEs. For example, 32MB or 64MB of memory is now obtainable on many consumer level computers.

The other component is called ROM. ROM stands for 'Read-Only-Memory'. ROM is an integrated circuit and chip-set. At the factory the computer manufacturer stores a zillion binary pre-coded BIT streams in the ROM chip. These ROM BITs are "hardwired" in the sense that the BITs are pre-set through how the circuitry is configured. That is, the circuits come up in a specific order and the very same order each and every time the computer is turned on. The electricity first flows into these ROM circuits and actuates the pre-coded order of BITs.

This particular set of BITs, sometimes called the "Initial Program Load" or IPL is 'streamed' or transferred at nearly the speed of light into memory. After loading into memory, it sets off several utility programs stored on the hard disk to 'boot-up' the computer, including loading the computer's operating system. The end of the "boot-up" process is actually the point at which a user can begin to run any and all applications.

You may wonder how the computer, after being "locked up", can be restarted, and the user can "Start" again any of the available software. The ROM chip is the answer. It is pre-programmed to come up with the same sequence or order of "Startup" BITs every time the computer is "booted" up. It is called 'Read-Only-Memory" because it can never be overwritten by mistake by the user. So no matter how many times we users may screw up our files, or our installed software, a restart of the computer will bring us back to the "Start" point by loading the "startup" programs into active memory.

The fact that ROM always comes back to life upon restart means that we can characterize it as "non-volatile" in contrast to memory. So it can be accurately stated that primary storage has both 'volatile' and 'non-volatile' components. And these components are memory and ROM respectively. ROM is what makes the computer truly "idiot proof". No matter how badly you screwed up, for the most part, you can always restart the computer which then reloads the IPLs and operating system and enables you to start again. Memory should not be confused with ROM. ROM unlike memory is non-volatile.

The mere wording of the computer's various components is a factor which defies the learning curve. Few people ever refer to memory as main memory or "primary storage" anymore. And it appears that we are evolving socially with simply "memory". Computer ads now still use RAM to indicate memory to a large extent, both in written media and always in radio and TV commercials.

Memory Has Limits

When you "open" a file stored on your computer's disk, the file is transferred at the BIT level to memory. As we said earlier, memory is "active" memory. The file would need to be stored here to permit you to actively work on it. The more files you are working on or transferring to memory, the more work you can process.

Now memory has limits. And this is one of the most important elements to understand about memory. You can only transfer and store in memory up to the amount of memory that is installed on your computer. The amount of memory is measured in BYTEs. The more memory BYTEs on your computer, the more you can store in active memory, and the more powerful your computer will be. This is because memory is dynamic and fast.

Everything stored in memory is directly accessible at nearly the speed of light. Many factors at the machine level can be implemented to 'speed-up' memory access. For example, software can be used to create things called 'arrays' and 'tables' which optimize the storage of BYTEs in active memory. But programming memory is beyond the scope of this book.

Many people still fear that if they touch the computer they will break it. Sort of like some people have a fear of holding a baby. Having to do a restart is perhaps the only "worst-case" scenario I can think of, and this is something that takes a minute. Computers are restarted all the time for many various reasons. Restarting is common among the computer literate, programmers and the like, as well as novices. So don't even be concerned about it. Now if you get it in your mind that you should be taking the processor box apart and yanking the ROM chip for observation, then I would say you are probably heading in the wrong direction, generally speaking, of course.

It is also crucially important for you to understand that we measure primary storage, specifically memory in you guessed it— BYTEs. This is very important to remember, because you will need at times to make decisions about what kind of computer to procure. And what kind of computer to use to run various applications which are important to you. Memory is active memory. Memory is one of those 'power factors' I refer to on the computer. The more memory you have onboard your computer, the faster your applications will run and the more applications you will be able to load concurrently. Concurrent loading makes application life more enjoyable. Imagine if you had to shutdown each application every time you wanted to use a different application. It would get frustrating.

BYTEs Now Have Standard Abbreviations

I summarize below the "de facto standard" acronyms which have evolved to measure memory in BYTEs. Like the bps de facto standards from Part I, these have evolved in the exact same way. That is through continuing use and evolution of the technology. So when you evaluate capacities for memory, hard disk, diskette, CD-ROM, and whatever new secondary storage devices come along, know these well. And they are:

Byte Abbreviations

B	BYTE
KB	KiloBYTE or thousand BYTEs
MB	Mega or million BYTEs
GB	Giga or billion BYTEs
TB	Tera or trillion BYTEs

You may notice that I'm using all upper-case characters. For instance, we have "B, KB, MB, GB and TB". Indeed this is the intent of the de facto standard. And many companies that manufacture computer and related technology use these acronyms to illustrate in abbreviated form the power of their products. Companies also use, along with the BYTE indicators, the BITs-per-second or bps abbreviation. (The de facto standard for BITs is to use the lower case b. For example Kb or Kbps, Mb or Mbps and so on.)

What happens frequently is that people get the two confused, and it becomes difficult to determine if we are talking BITs or BYTEs. Obviously, with as much as a 16 to 1 difference between the number of BITs per character BYTE, this could get out of control. Vendors could intentionally or non-intentionally misstate the power of their products. Therefore I am strongly in favor of moving from the de facto to the formally defined standardization of these two important elements of the computer generation, namely BITs and BYTEs.

Imagine reviewing the specification sheet on a piece of hardware which states that memory chips come with 128K or 128Kb on a computer that you were considering for purchase. This could be misleading. This could mean 128,000 BYTEs or 128,000 BITs depending on our definition or abbreviation of the BIT & BYTE. And today for another example, modems are being advertised as 56K. What little clarity we had with the de facto standard meanings appears to be eroding. 56K can imply 56,000 BYTEs. But the factual reality is that it means 56,000 BITs-per-second.

Moving forward to secondary storage, I'll summarize by saying that the importance of Primary storage to the power of a computer is inestimable. ROM is required to enable the computer each and every time the computer is started. The amount of memory, and memory is made up of millions of addressable units, legitimately referred to as

BYTEs or BYTE-size cells, determines how much you can load in your computer at any given time to work on. The more free memory you have the more software application files you can load. And lastly, memory, measured in BYTEs, works together with the Data BUS, clock speed and the size and type of instruction set to determine the computer's power as measured in characteristics such as "MIPS" or millions of instructions per second.

Secondary Storage: Where BYTEs Take Up Permanent Residence

Now that we have clarified where, for the most part, the power of a computer comes from, at least from the "internal processing" perspective, it is time to move onward and upward to secondary storage. Secondary storage enables us to 'store' the BITs which make-up the BYTEs over the long-haul. Particularly, after you power-off your computer. I refer to this as BYTEs inhabiting the hard disk.

As we discussed, primary storage is 'volatile'. When you power-off or lose power to your computer "primary storage' is zeroed out, becoming completely "off-state". But, as you process various applications using word-processing, spreadsheeting, graphical, database and any one of 1000s of different software packages, part of your procedure(s), if you are using the computer technology correctly, exhort you to "save" your data on any one of various media in the category of secondary storage.

Secondary storage enables us computer users to save over time, all of the data we temporarily store in memory. So that at subsequent times, we can continue to work on our data by picking up where we left off. We can maintain historical records of the data with which we work, we can readily recall, for example, previous e-mail messages we may have sent, or graphical images we may have used. In addition we can provide electronic versions of work that we may need to submit to others who then would electronically add their respective parts and forward on to the next person. These are just a few of the things which secondary storage facilitates over time.

Secondary storage, similar to primary storage is a beautiful thing. Like memory, secondary storage is measured in BYTEs . Unlike memory, however, it has become dirt-cheap. Less than .10¢ per MB. That is less than ten cents for One MegaBYTE or One Million BYTEs. And getting cheaper. Secondary storage has become nearly limitless in today's computer world.

One standard 8.5" by 11" page of paper can hold approximately 4,000 BYTEs on it. That is, if every possible space on the page is used. Now, if you calculate how many pages of information you could store in secondary storage for .10¢, it adds up to about 250 pages. If I said, "you could store about 250 pages of information for less than a dime" would you be impressed, economically or otherwise? And the price is coming down as more effective technological ways of storing and retrieving are developed.

Currently the 10¢ metric does not include the latest and greatest "writable CD technology". Writable CDs or "Writable Optical Storage" are real hot right now. You may have heard of CD-ROM type of secondary storage, which is now being used extensively to deploy software at all levels, shapes and sizes. CD-ROM technology though is "read-only". That is, you can read CD-ROM into memory to use, install on your hard-disk, display on your computer, but you cannot store anything on the CD-ROM platter.

Though the technology is in place to enable "writing" to CDs, it has yet to become cost-effective for the individual computer consumer. However, as with any new technology, when it first comes out, it is relatively expensive. After it works its way through the market over time, competition kicks in, customer feedback kicks in, and we have proportional efficiencies incorporated into the packaging and deployment, such that the technology becomes cheaper. More people buy. The price comes down over time. The same process can be seen historically with most technologies. The same is occurring with writable CDs.

By the way, CD technology uses laser optics to do its thing to encode the equivalent of the "ON" and the "OFF" states, or if you please, the "HIGH and the "LOW" light pulse codes onto the CD platter. Computer software manufacturers use writable CDs extensively to sell their software to consumers. They can afford the high cost of the writable CD devices. But they pass the proportional cost on to the consumer.

The consumer gets the CD in the form of a 'read-only' disk or platter. Standard CD-ROM disk platters are 5" in diameter and hold a minimum of 500MB per platter. The consumer merely needs to have a computer system that can read a CD and install or load its contents onto the consumer's 'hard disk'. The hard disk employs electro-magnetic principles to encode the "ON" and "OFF" states (HIGH or LOW pulse codes) onto the disk platter compared to the laser light optical pulse codes methods of the CD technology.

Secondary storage typically is not considered a major power factor. This is because it has become dirt-cheap. And secondary storage does not usually play a major role in the real-time operation of the computer. It kicks in whenever the computer needs to recall, (retrieve), store, (save) permanently, information currently active in memory. BYTE information files can also be copied from one secondary storage device to another. Such as, from the hard disk to the diskette, or vice-versa.

Secondary storage does play an important role in supporting the installation of various software onto the computer. It is in secondary storage where the installed software "takes up residence" (i.e.inhabits), and therefore can be recalled for operational use at any time the computer user wants to use it. This includes the operating system software necessary for integration and control of the computer system.

Smaller, Cheaper, Faster and Better Storage

When we consider secondary storage today, it generally indicates that we are talking about the 'hard drive'. And it is typical today to characterize the computer's hard-drive by its total storage capacity as expressed in BYTEs. For example: 8GB, or 8-gigabyte hard disk.

Other factors play a role in assessing the 'Hard Drive's' speed. Such as, "What type of 'interface' come with it?" More technical users would ask this type of question. The speed of the hard drives can also refer to the interface which connects the 'Hard Disk' to the computer's motherboard.

Discussion of secondary storage device interfaces reeks of technical jargon, which will take us where we don't want to go. Therefore I would like you to realize that there are varying types of interfaces to connect secondary storage devices to the computer's main Data BUS. They vary in cost and speed. Smaller, cheaper, faster, and presumably better, lives on.

Like all computer technology, the size of secondary storage devices has and will continue to get smaller. And the physical size of the 'Hard Disk' has gotten much smaller. My Notebook PC has a 2GB 'Hard Disk' and is 3" by 2 " and .5" wide. My hard drive fits snugly into a slot on my Notebook. And my Notebook is a model that has been on the market for about 2 years.

For now it is a safe bet that most Notebook Computers and PCs today are shipping with at least the standard 3.5" drive, and a GB capacity Hard Drive/Disk. A majority of PCs and Notebooks selling today also have a CD-ROM or at least the option for one. On my Notebook I have a slot for my 3.5" diskette drive. I also have, and can replace, the diskette drive with a CD-ROM drive by simply powering off the computer and swapping the devices. The diskette drive and CD-ROM drive share the same slot, but in my case, not concurrently.

Most recently in 1998 we now have available the SuperDisk. It is a 3.5" diskette but can hold 120MBs. Or multiply by 83 the capacity of, if I may say, the old 3.5" diskette. The newer 250MB capacity Zip disk is outpacing the 120MB Zip Disk. It is due out in January 1999.

There is now a full range of CD-ROM options with varying drive speeds and capacities. Writable CDs are expected to be consumer ready in the near future. They are on the market now, but cost is still high. You can buy the writable discs. But remember, you need to have the writable drive on your computer. The drive is the expensive piece.

Summarizing Secondary Storage

In summarizing secondary storage the first and foremost element of knowledge that computer users need to understand is that it can store or retain the information and software used on your computer permanently. It does its secondary storage thing fundamentally by storing in BYTEs. These BYTEs are further organized into what are known as 'Files'.

- Secondary storage is characterized as "non-volatile", meaning that the information and software saved in secondary storage is immediately and directly retrievable when the computer is restarted for subsequent sessions. This is why it is recommended that computer users "save" their work periodically on secondary storage, because if ever there were a power supply interruption to your computer, all information since your last "save" would be lost.
- Secondary storage does not depend or rely entirely on pure slectricity to operate, as is the case with volatile memory. The hard disk operates on electro-magnetic principles, same as the diskette. And the CD-ROM storage operates on electro-optical principles.
- There are three components to consider in comprehending any secondary storage subsystem. First the "storage medium" is not the exact same thing as the "storage device". Let me explain. I have a hard disk which is the storage medium installed at the factory on my computer. The hard disk is installed in a device known as the "hard disk drive". The "hard disk drive" is connected into the motherboard and thus to the main Data BUS.
- Diskette storage has the same three components. The storage medium is the diskette itself. The diskette is inserted into the "Diskette Drive" for storage or retrieval of information. The "diskette drive" is connected to the motherboard and thus to the main Data BUS.
- Ditto for the CD-ROM. There is the medium, which is the CD-ROM platter disk itself. There is a "CD-ROM disk drive". The "CD-ROM disk drive" is connected to the motherboard and thus the main Data BUS.
- Secondary storage plays an important role in the overall operation of the computer. Secondary storage like primary storage is measured in BYTEs. Secondary storage is cheap and getting cheaper. Writable CD disks, the 3.5" Superdisk, and the newer Zip disks are the latest technologies to revolutionize the domain of secondary storage. It continues to get smaller, cheaper, faster and better.

9

The BYTE and the File

In our discussion of memory we, illustrated the point that a BYTE is made up of one or more BITs, depending on what kind of BYTE we are working with. Mathematical BYTEs are calculated in the Arithmetic Logic Unit (ALU) and concurrently are stored in active memory in BYTE-size cells. The number of BYTEs (or memory cells) required to store a calculated number in memory depends on the size and length of the number. It will take more memory cells to hold a number like 6 million than it will to hold a simple number like 6.

With the non-mathematical, keystrokes are encoded directly into BYTEs, based on the computer's preinstalled standardized character set, such as ASCII, EBCDIC or UNICODE. ASCII uses a 7-BIT code and EBCDIC uses an 8-BIT code to construct letters and other characters. UNICODE uses a 16-BIT code. The UNICODE incorporates completely the entire character sets and corresponding binary codes for all of the characters contained in the ASCII and EBCDIC Standard Coding Systems along with the corresponding binary codes for every character in every language of the world. This enables any computer running UNICODE to support any natural language in the world!

BITs Form BYTEs, BYTEs Form Files

Even though operating at nearly the speed of light, if the computer organized its BIT transfers and BYTE "savings" at the BIT level, that is BIT by BIT, it would be an ominous task even for the computer to process and store information. After all, we are talking about a system that requires at least 8 to 16 BITs just to process one single letter. And for the mathematical types of information, the BYTE storage requirements are directly tied to the size of the number expressed in its binary form. So, mathematical BYTE storage requirements could be enormous.

Part of the magic and power of moving BITs and BYTEs is in organizing the large quantities of BITs and BYTEs into much larger units. The computer can and will transfer as little as 1 single BIT per instance. But typically, computer users work with application software which processes large groups of BITs, which are BYTE-a-sized by the software. By this I mean that even though at the lowest level everything is BITs, using an application software package-any software package-means that the computer will be made to "organize" all of the BITs & BYTEs to be transferred within the computer. Application software organizes BYTEs in a specific order. This BYTE-ordering results in the creation and storage by the application software of units we call "files". Files are measured in BYTEs.

Application software, working through the computer's circuitry, translates automatically and transparently to you, the user, the BITs into BYTEs, whether they be mathematical BYTEs or nonmathematical BYTEs. It further organizes these BYTE-elements into larger units that are referred to as files. The computer user merely follows the respective procedures that go along with the given application software package. The application software takes care of the accompanying details needed for organizing BITs and BYTEs into files.

Every application software package necessarily must organize the BITs and BYTEs the user is processing based on the users specific requirements. This usually pans out in the form of a user creating one or more files. Instead of moving a zillion individual BITs, one BIT at a time, the computer organizes its BIT transfers into units called files. When the computer transfers BITs, it first translates the file into a 'BIT Stream'. The organized BIT stream is then transferred. Upon reaching its destination the BIT stream gets translated back into a file.

Files are transferred all the time in support of computer users. When you make a word-processing document it is created in memory using the word-processing software package of your choice. However, when you name and save the document, the computer's operating system makes it a file. And the file takes up physical presence, or, you might say, it "takes up residence" on your secondary storage media of choice under the file name you the user assign. For most computer users, the choice of storage location is either the hard disk or the diskette.

The name of the file becomes a critical factor in managing your computer system. Imagine the number and type of files a computer user will create over time. Now imagine the total BYTE storage requirements that can accumulate over time. How you name your files becomes directly related to how you can subsequently retrieve them. Relevant and easy names will make it easier to remember and easier to recall the files, generally speaking.

The size of a file is measured in BYTEs. Memory is measured in BYTEs. The size of the file in BYTEs becomes an issue when you have limited BYTE-space on your computer, either BYTE-space in memory or on your secondary storage. The size of the files you have stored is an issue in performance. The larger the BYTE-size of your files the longer it will take to open, save, print, download and upload.

Moreover, large files can increase contention on your computer and your computer network, if these resources are not adequately designed to handle large files. (Contention is traffic congestion. That is, too much data on the main data BUS of your computer or on the network you may be connected to). The key is 'adequate design'. If you can envision the need to move a lot of large files, say files in excess of 1MB in size, then you may want to consider having optimal amounts of memory and secondary storage.

What is optimal? You could count up and project out how many total BYTEs you will need based on that projection. If you are planning to move files in excess of 20MB in capacity, for example, you can see right away that if you have only 16MB of memory, that you are not going to be able to load the entire file into active memory. This means that your use of the application software and its accompanying data files will be less than adequate.

And there is a corresponding need to project not only how much memory in total BYTEs you are going to need, but also a need to determine how much secondary storage will be required. Like memory, secondary storage such as the hard disk and diskette are measured in total BYTEs as well. When estimating your secondary storage needs, take into account all the many and varied application software packages you are going to be installing and using on your computer. These software packages inhabit or take up residence typically on your computer's hard disk.

Everything moves in files on the computer. Files are made up of

BYTEs. And BYTEs are made up of BITs. And BITs can be the binary coding for one or more characters, each character in this case being a single BYTE. Or BITs can be the binary representation of one or more mathematical number(s), each number in this case being one or more BYTEs, depending on the size of the number involved.

File Extensions Are Key to Organization on the Computer

Organizing BITs into files is so important to the computer's operating system that 'File Extensions' must be assigned in order for the computer to distinguish among the various types of files that can be processed on a computer. Many 'file extensions' are used today. For example, to represent a COBOL progam file you might have a file name like PAYROLL.COB where the .COB is an extension that signifies to the operating system that this file is specifically a COBOL file. Files used in the programming language known as C++ have a File extension of C++. Database files typically have extensions like .DB or .MDB to represent database files. Another example is .BMP which is a file extension representing a BIT mapped file used in graphics applications. For every application software package you may use, the files created will have a unique file extension associated with it. This is how the operating system can distinguish, dispatch and organize the various Files coming in and out of the computer system.

I should emphasize that the application software being used along with the computer's operating system software (i.e. WINDOWS, 95, NT, etc.) takes care of assigning file extensions to files. So file extension assignments happen transparently behind the scenes. But it is useful to be aware of file extensions because there will be times when you, the user, will get confused or may be in a hurry and click on opening the wrong type of file for the application software you are using. It happens and it is easy to do. When you do, you will get an error message on the display indicating the incompatibility. The operating system is calling the file you specified, but when it goes to load it into memory under the application software you are using it finds that it cannot be loaded due to a mismatch in the file extension. An example would be like trying to open directly a .BMP file into an EXCEL spreadsheet application which looks for a .XLS file extension.

Other Levels of File Organization

On the computer, files, depending on the application system software can also grow into other higher levels of organization or 'storage units'. Database software, at its core, is application software that is a master of organizing many bazillions of BYTEs into files. It does this by further organizing BYTEs into fields. Then fields into larger units we call 'records'. And then records are contained in files. In its most fundamental form, a database is essentially a method for organizing more stringently, one or more files, and then interconnecting the files that make up the database.

Databases are real hot items in today's world. All sectors of society are using databases to store and retrieve information on a wide range of subjects. And databases come down to being one or more files, which are stored on the computer's secondary storage, or on some secondary storage device located on the network. When needed, the database software is executed and loaded into memory. When the user calls for required information, the database software takes care of loading into memory which files are needed for use from the appropriate secondary storage device.

With respect to database software, there is a hierarchy, which illustrates the size-magnitude and relationship of BITs and BYTEs to the larger storage units such as files and databases. We just don't go from BYTE to database. In between, we have the other "sizing units" of which you need to be aware.

First there is the BIT in all of its 'ON' or 'OFF' splendor. So many BITs, make up the BYTE. As discussed, the BYTE can either be a mathematical or a nonmathematical BYTE. (You may also surmise here that the BYTE can correspond to a letter, number or special character.)

When we are talking databases, the next incremental unit employed for organizing the BITs and BYTEs is called a 'field'. Another name used for field is an 'attribute'. So many BYTEs make up a field or attribute. Once a group of BYTEs become a field, the field takes on a name. Two of the most common field names in databases are the SSN or Social Security Number and the Name field.

Call your telephone banking service center or any credit card servicing center and you will see this fact played out. The representative answering will, 9 out of 10 times verify who you are by asking you for SSN or your Name. They also either will ask or determine through their database software your account number. Account number is yet another example of a database field. Of course, you can surmise that the representative is, in this example, working on the computer with the company's database software.

To organize further the BITs and BYTEs into yet larger units of storage, the field or attributes of a file are organized into specific groups known as 'Records'. A record is a group of related field(s). So in the example above, it perhaps would be appropriate for the database that the representative is using to have an "account record" for each and every customer.

The length or number of BYTEs in a given record is something which can and does vary from database to database. Ditto this for the size and number of fields per record. These elements are a function of the design of the database. But once the BYTE length is determined, it remains the same, for the most part. For example, the SSN field will generally be 9 individual numbers, or BYTEs, long. And if the design of the database calls for inclusion of the two dashes in the SSN, then the field could be designed to hold a total of 11 BYTEs.

So many records make up a file. And all of the records in a file have the same field or attributes in common. So that if an account record exists for one person in a file, each and every other record in that file will be an account record for each and every customer. And each and every record will have the exact same number and type of field or attributes.

Lastly, all databases are made up of one or more files. Yes a database can have only one, single file. Usually, though, a database has multiple files. All files in a database are related in some way through the records that make up the various files. For example, the database above might include an account file, registration file and a history file. Each of these files in the database are linked by some common field such as SSN. Database software links related files.

Corporate Databases Typically Have Many Files

Database files are the most organized files on a computer system. There is clearly a hierarchy from the low level and smallest of storage units, namely BITs and BYTEs, on up through the actual storage method known as the database. This order, including field or attributes, records and files is necessary for the computer to control the access and updating of the information contained therein.

Although popular, database files are not the only types of file that are stored and processed on a computer. Though they are at this point with the continuing evolution of the computer-the most organized.

Inside the computer at the BIT level, a file is simply a container that can have huge numbers of BITs in it. The application software takes care of creating and organizing files on the computer. Whether they be database files with other levels or units of storage which make up the file, or any other type of file, your application software does the grunt work for you.

The important concepts to remember here are that BITs become BYTEs. BYTEs get organized into larger units of storage called files. Other units of storage can be employed like fields and records by such software as in databases or graphics applications, but the fundamental unit of storage beyond the singular BYTE is the file. Finally, files are measured in BYTEs, just like memory and all other forms of storage.

File Dynamics Between Primary and Secondary Storage

To this point we have covered how BYTEs become stored temporarily in memory. And we have discussed how BYTEs are stored permanently in secondary storage. What would be useful for us is to now turn to what would be the interaction that takes place between these two forms of storage. This will reinforce your knowledge of both forms of storage and illustrate how we get things done on the computer.

Given that ROM is a requirement for "boot-up" and is really static in the sense that it is set at the factory and does what it does each and every time we turn on the computer, we really do not need to go any further with ROM. So I'll leave ROM with the statement that when we do turn on the computer, the Initial Program Load or IPL which we discussed earlier, is loaded into memory. The IPL calls for the operating system that is typically preinstalled in secondary storage on the hard disk. As such, the IPLs coming from ROM take up BYTE space in active memory. This is important to understand. That said, we can leave ROM and move to the operating system.

Typically the operating system (OS) software comes with the computer system. Upon installation of the OS software it takes up residence in secondary storage on the hard disk. The OS is called up by the IPLs and retrieved from secondary each and every time the computer is started. The OS is copied from secondary storage into memory where it becomes active in support of the entire computer system. We need the operating system loaded in memory in order to load whatever application software we will be using. The OS is an extremely important part of your computer system. It controls the integration and operations of your computer system. It is important to realize that it is both stored permanently in secondary storage and loaded temporarily into memory on startup. The OS takes a set amount of 'BYTE' capacity in order to be stored on hard disk. The OS also requires BYTE storage capacity in memory to support subsequent applications that may be selected by the user after the computer is started.

Following is an illustration showing how memory gets stacked from startup to the point where a user can be concurrently running several applications:

Illustration of What Gets Stacked Into Main Memory

Loading Sequences	**Software Item**	**Required**	**Memory Amount***	**Loaded From**
First	IPLs	Yes	50KB	ROM
Second	OS	Yes	120KB	Disk
Third	Word-Processing	Selectable	240KB	Disk
Fourth	Spreadsheeting	Selectable	275KB	Disk
Fifth	E-mail	Selectable	240KB	Disk
Sixth	Database	Selectable	295KB	Disk
		Total Storage	1.22MB	

**generic typical estimate, total BYTE-count will vary by system and software*

Upon loading of the OS, we are now ready to start work on one or more of the application software packages we may have installed. Being installed means that this software was loaded into secondary storage, usually the hard disk, and usually from a CD-ROM or 3 _" diskette(s)at a previous time. Under the supervision of the operating system software which is loaded beforehand when the computer is turned on, the application software enables you to complete the various tasks that you may need to work on, including creating various files, printing, e-mail, etc. It is important to realize that like the OS software, application software is stored permanently in secondary storage and copied temporarily into memory at the time that the user selects it. For example, when users click on their e-mail Icon, the program to run e-mail is then loaded into memory. The user is presented with the screen to do e-mail.

As we work with the application software we end up creating one or more files which initially are stored in memory. When we save our file and assign a file name, the file remains in its temporary location in memory, but concurrently an exact duplicate is copied into secondary storage. If the file already exists on secondary storage, that is, on your disk, the OS software typically will prompt you, via the screen, with a message such as, "This file already exists. Do you want to replace it? Yes or No?". If you say, "Yes", the current version of the file in memory overwrites the previous version stored on your disk. If "No", then the command is cancelled.

The location in secondary storage is something that the user can select as part of the procedure for saving files to secondary storage. So, for example, you can specify that a file presently in memory be saved (copied) to the hard disk or to a diskette. Or you can save (copy) the file from memory to just the hard disk. When complete, you may elect to save (copy) the same file from memory to only the diskette. In this way, you have 2 copies of the same file in two separate physical locations, namely the hard disk and the diskette. (Neat for backup copies and flexibility).

What is important here, first, is to understand the distinction between memory which is temporary, dynamic storage and its inexorable relationship with permanent, secondary storage, hard disk or diskette, usually referred to as the disk.

One is active and volatile; namely memory. And the other is static and non-volatile; namely the disk.

Moreover, anything that is loaded into memory takes up space measured in 'BYTEs'. You need to know this so you can manage your computer system. The more you need to load into memory, the more memory you may need. This is measured again in BYTEs.

And remember, that regardless of the number and type of application software packages you will be loading, any computer requires the ROM IPLs to be loaded first upon booting up the computer. During boot-up, IPL loading is followed by the loading of the OS software. These two elements alone will take up a significant part of your Memory.

Furthermore, know the BYTE storage requirements of your application software packages, when these software packages load into memory and how many BYTEs each package will require to take up residence on your disk. Usually these 2 storage requirements will vary. That is, a package usually takes up more BYTEs to store on disk than it does to load into memory. The reason is that there are options for what parts of the software package get loaded into memory. In other words, the entire BYTE capacity of a software package does not typically need to be loaded into memory in order for you to use the package.

Never skimp on the amount of memory you buy. Memory is where it's at. Active memory! This is where everything gets processed on input and transformed for output. If you skimp and expect to overload your memory, the computer's performance will suffer greatly. You will become frustrated. You could have problems completing procedures like 'saving a file to disk' or printing a hardcopy. What eventually gets saved on disk may not be what you needed to have saved. Optimal memory means optimal computer performance.

Everything stored on a computer system, that is, any secondary storage device such as hard disk or a diskette or even in memory, gets there in the form of what we have come to call files. Files, files, files and more files. This means huge amounts of BYTEs organized into an electronic container, which we are calling a file.

All files have some type of extension to distinguish the specific software that was used to create the file. The OS uses the file extension to manage everything having to do with the file. The OS must key on the file extension whenever the user saves, retrieves, modifies, copies, transfers or prints a file.

A file extension is typically a 3-character abbreviation that gets appended to the actual name assigned to the file. For example .DOC corresponds to a document file created by word-processing software. The word-processing software working with the operating system software automatically assigns the file extension.

When we install any application software package on our computer, the process of installing necessarily loads and stores onto the hard disk many files. These files vary in length and type. But they share the commonality of being necessary for the delivery of the many and varied features of the particular application software package being installed.

The same file process holds up for the installing of the operating system software (OS) as well. The result of installing the OS software results in several, you guessed it, files, being stored on the hard disk. Although the OS files are not typically viewed as application files, OS files do perform many functions in support of the computer user's needs. Things like saving, copying and deleting files are just some of the many functions performed by the OS. On a computer system we have application software files. Application software permits the user to create other files, known as 'user-defined' or 'user-created' files. We also have OS files. Following is an illustration of a startup involving: OS, application and user files:

Illustration of What Gets Stacked Into Main Memory

Loading Sequences	Software Item	Required	Memory Amount*	Loaded From
First	IPLs	Yes	50KB	ROM
Second	OS	Yes	120KB	Disk
Third	Word-Processing	Selectable	240KB	Disk
Fourth	Spreadsheeting	Selectable	275KB	Disk
Fifth	E-mail	Selectable	240KB	Disk
Sixth	Database	Selectable	295KB	Disk
Seventh	File .DOC	User Created	Variable**	Disk.
Eighth	File .XLS	User Created	Variable**	Disk
Ninth	File .XCH	User Created	Variable**	Disk
Tenth	File .MDB	User Created	Variable**	Disk
		Total Storage	1.22MB+	

*generic typical estimate **limited by amount of memory

Both types of files, application software (user) and operating system (system) files are stored permanently on secondary storage, typically the hard disk. Files are retrieved when appropriate and or when user selects them, from secondary storage and loaded into active memory, when needed.

There is yet another type of file of which you need to be aware. These are the files that result from our working on the computer to create and modify files. These files are called typically 'data' files. And when created and saved are assigned a file extension which typically corresponds to the specific application software being used during file creation.

Some applications have several different file types under their control. Database software packages have as many as 8 to 10 or more different file extensions that apply to the various features and functions of the software package. Database software lets you create screen forms, query screens, table data structures and other file types. The point here is that each of these different functions requires one or more files. In order to distinguish these various files, the file extension is assigned by the application software to each file when the file is created and assigned a file name. (File name is not the same as file extension.)

When we use the word-processing application software this usually results in the creation of one or more "word-processing" 'documents. These documents actually become files when the user saves them on disk and assigns a file name to them. At that time the application software in cooperation with the computer's operating system, although transparent to you, the user, also assigns a file extension. And the same goes for any other application software package. What changes are that different, unique file extensions are assigned by different application software packages? But a unique file extension nevertheless will be assigned. And the OS uses the extension to distinguish among the many and varied files it must track.

For another example, when we use the spreadsheeting application software, this usually results in the creation of one or more spreadsheets. These spreadsheets become files with a unique file name assignment once the user saves the spreadsheet(s) on the disk. Again the application software in cooperation with the OS assigns the file extension.

Other application software can be used and not necessarily result in the creation of a file. If you are browsing the WEB using your WEB browsing application software, you are mainly cruising the WEB and checking things out. Sometimes you may want to save on your disk information that you may find at a particular WEB site. We call this "downloading" a file from the WEB. If you do a download, you essentially would be saving a file (that is, the downloaded file) on your disk and assigning a file name. And, again, the OS in cooperation with your WEB browser software would assign an extension to the file name you assign.

The whole point here is that in addition to OS and application software files, which pretty much get installed, loaded in memory when needed, and take up residence on your computer's hard disk, we computer users generate other types of files from using the OS and application software. These "other" files are called "data" files or "user-defined files". Data or user-defined files, like all files, are measured in BYTEs and are used to feed application software.

So, if you maintain the company's or the household's budget on a computer using your spreadsheet software, you would save this information in a data-file and maintain this file over time on your hard disk. Or, at work you may be required to store (save) such a file on the company file server's hard disk. In this way you can subsequently retrieve and modify the spreadsheet as conditions change.

You can also elect to retrieve the file to make current modifications based on the latest information and save the spreadsheet under a new file name assignment. This action keeps your original spreadsheet intact and creates an additional copy with the latest information under a new name. And you could maintain these and all other subsequent versions of the budget in this manner. In this way you could retrospectively evaluate all previous budgets.

Data files of all BYTE sizes and types are maintained typically on the hard disk. Data files typically grow in BYTE size over time as we users modify them and resave them on disk. Files can become "bloated" to the point where they take up inordinate amounts of BYTE space, both on disk and in memory. When this happens it first of all is important to understand what is happening. Second, depending on what type of file, that is, what type of application software was used to create the file, the user may have options for making the file more efficient.

In terms relative to the Y2K set of problems, the file really does not care if the year is expressed in 2-BYTEs or 4-BYTEs. The application software you are using will determine how many BYTEs will be stored in the file. Several techniques are used for adjusting to and resolving how the calendar-year-related BYTEs contained in a file could be processed correctly. I detail these techniques in Part IV.

Also, the Y2K problem descriptions you will generally hear in the media refer to a 2-digit year versus a 4-digit year. A digit in this case is the exact equivalent of 1-BYTE. So, Y2K in its simplest form is a problem, between expressing the year as a 2-BYTE field versus a 4-BYTE field. How these BYTEs may be subsequently stored in a file is only indirectly related to how these BYTEs are initially captured (i.e. entered), and how these BYTEs are processed after the related file reaches its destination to be processed.

Some software packages come with features for users to "compress" the size of a file. Basically compression enables you to shrink the size of the file for secondary storage purposes, while keeping its essential BYTE information and the order of this information intact.

Furthermore, today on the market we have software packages that can read through a file and automatically update (i.e. remediate) the calendar year fields. This new software has greatly reduced the cost generally with fixing the software component of the Y2K set of problems.

Other file management techniques include "splitting" the file into one or more parts. The technical term for this is "partitioning", and storing (saving) the files on different secondary storage mediums. For example, some files could be on hard disk, some on diskette. Or even in the case of being on a network, store the files on a computer server hard disk.

Computer servers are essentially computers with optimal Data BUS size, clock speed, memory and very large BYTE-size and usually multiple hard disk(s). These servers are typically called 'File Server(s)' because their main purpose in computer network life is to use the computer network to support many of the computer users on the network by permitting these users to save and retrieve many different types and sizes of files which are stored on its hard disk(s).

Today the cost of secondary storage, at least hard disk and diskette, has become very cheap. Still, the cost of memory or main memory is not quite as cheap. And more importantly, the size of the file impacts performance operations. That is, the speed of your application software. If your word-processing software has to digest a bloated file in excess, say of 1MB, you will see that there will be some obvious delays, even on computers that have maximum amounts of memory on-board.

In cases where there may be limited amounts of memory or disk space on the computer, delays will be exacerbated. And on computers with non-current software, say an older version of the OS or an older version of the application software, trying to run on a computer with the most current OS, you may not only have delays but incompatibilities in operations. The computer may not function completely. Or it may work only partially.

At this point we have covered how ON and OFF states become BYTEs, mathematically and non-mathematically. BYTEs are processed in memory in containers that we call files. Files take up residence in the form of output when we assign names to files and save the files as output to secondary storage. Files are assigned file extensions by the application software in cooperation with the computer's OS. File name, along with file extension, uniquely identifies a given file to the computer system and all of its software. Thus, we can subsequently retrieve from permanent storage and work on files as our needs change. Lastly, all files, regardless of type, are measured in total BYTEs.

We now turn to other forms of output which are more visible to us, namely the monitor display and the hardcopy printer.

10

The BYTE and Output: WYSIWYG

The title really says it all. If only it were that simple. But, essentially, if we can generate a BYTE we can see it on our monitor display. Or, we could print it out on a printer. Thus, we can apply this same 'BYTE principal' to larger groups of BYTEs, such as files of all sizes and types, including word-processing documents, spreadsheeets, e-mail messages and so on.

What complicates this discussion is that there are so many types, shapes, sizes, styles and brands of both monitors and printers. To inventory all of the many flavors of monitors and printers is a project beyond the scope of this book. It is more important to me that you understand the essential elements of display devices and printers from a BYTE perspective, so that you can manage your own use of these components and perhaps assist others that may be struggling with them. If we can see it in BYTE form on the screen display, it can be outputted to a printer.

Monitors

One thing to remember about monitors is that they are considered to be in the category of computer hardware. Monitors connect into the computer's Data BUS via the motherboard. When you press keys on the keyboard, the same BYTE translations occur, and BYTEs are concurrently stored in memory while also appearing on the monitor's screen display. This means that if you see it on the monitor screen it is also active and resident in the computer's memory.

A monitor is the type of hardware device which also has its own BUS known as the video-BUS. And the size of the video-BUS, like the main Data BUS is measured in BITs or BIT-width. The purpose of the video-BUS is the same as the purpose of the main Data BUS, except that the video-BUS confines itself strictly to processing BITs on the video-BUS and completing the interface to the computer's main Data BUS.

The video BUS comes hardwired into a section of the motherboard. A connection port is provided for the monitor. Usually you can see this port connection at the back of the processor box.

Speed of the monitor display used to be a major consideration in the purchase of a monitor. Because the video BUS size or width is measured in BITs, monitor speed is a function of video BUS size. However, monitor product pricing has come way down, like all computer-related technology will do. What has happened, however, since the early 90s is that specialty monitors have become a commodity product. As such, what used to be the fast, high-end monitors are now bundled in with the purchase of the computer system.

Up until 1994, computer systems would always be advertised as "monitor sold separately". This would usually result in an increase of $300-$700 to the final cost of the system, depending on how spiffy of a monitor you wanted. Today, computer systems are advertised to include the monitor. High-tech specialty monitors are negotiated separately.

So what is the difference between one monitor and the other? Mostly, it is the size. Sizes vary in inches. The range at the short end includes monitor displays for hand-held and notebook computers, 17" and 19" workstation displays used in desktop applications like computer animation and other graphics-related applications. In addition, we have monitor displays that can range up to wall size for specialized applications, like monitoring large computer networks. Imagine a wall-size screen that illustrates each connection point on a company's nationwide computer network.

More and more folks with mobile notebook computers with the smaller built-in display are using, in addition, the larger desktop screens for those times when they are at the desktop. The larger monitor simply connects into the video port on the back of the notebook. The video port is the motherboard's connection between the main

Data BUS and the video BUS. In this case the video BUS sends the same video signal translation to two separate destinations; namely the notebook's built-in screen and the larger screen of the plugged-in desktop monitor. This is possible because the machine level BITs and BYTEs, which make up the image, are stored in active RAM. Thus, these image(s) in RAM can easily be transported to any output device connected to the main Data BUS simultaneously.

In addition to size, monitors vary according to resolution or quality of display. Monitors use the technique of "Pixel Enlightenment" to do their stuff. Essentially, as the video BUS transmits the translated BYTEs on up to the screen for display, the BIT stream must pass through the monitors circuitry. The circuitry ends with the signals passing through the monitors "Pixel Board" which then becomes empowered with the appropriate image at the precise spot on the screen. Some images can, and most certainly do, take up more than one pixel. For example with a graphics image, you, the user, simply see the image or character appear on the screen. And if more than one monitor unit is connected to this computer's main Data BUS, then it is possible to place the same image display on the other monitor screens at the same time......well, say, within a few nanoseconds. (But we humans really won't notice any delay.)

The pixel count per BYTE is the major factor in determining quality of resolution. More pixels per BYTE means better quality or finer resolution on the screen. Cheap, low-end monitors tend to have a lower pixel-to-BYTE ratio. This ratio is expressed in 'mm', like .26mm or .28mm. The general computer consumer will not be readily aware of this unless they do some research prior to purchase. However, just by viewing and comparing, you can see differences in quality of resolution. You may not know that pixel count is behind what you see, but most folks can tell the quality of the monitor display by viewing it in comparison with other displays. The trick would be to make sure you view more than one type of monitor to see the difference. Generally, at this time in the marketplace, the consumer computer system bundles on the market come with a .28mm pixel count monitor.

Another important differentiator is color versus monochrome. Today, color monitors are sold mostly to consumers and desktop users. Monochrome displays are used for specialized applications where a cheap low-end display will suffice to meet display requirements.

Color in monitor displays is derived by manipulation of the BITs and BYTEs which makeup the screen display output. This manipulation is accomplished mainly through the software being used. However, the hardware makeup of the monitor device must support the kind of video software drivers being used.

Driver software is another term for computer software programs that are specific to accomplishing a single function. In this case, manipulation of the color on the screen displays. Remember, all software translates down to BITs. Video software is no exception. But video BITs translate back up to colorize pixels and the subsequent color display.

Of consideration just a few years ago would have been whether or not the monitor was interlaced or non-interlaced. Interlacing refers to the frame breaks on the screen. Did you ever view a monitor screen display in a movie? Used to be that you could see the breaks in the frame as they rolled out each consecutive display that produces the image we see. We viewers are not supposed to see this happening because it breaks up our image of the display into sequential frames, much like a movie film is broken up into consecutive frames.

Interlacing is what causes the monitor display to do this frame-breaking. And you could see the wide black lines rolling by indicating where the breaks were located; that is, if the monitor display was interlaced. If you're not sure what kind of monitor you are working with, view the screen from the sides of your eyes, or using your peripheral vision. If it is an interlaced monitor you will see the frame breaks rolling by. We see them in the movies because the movie actually is run for us at a speed that approximates the speed with which we need to see it, in order to have the perception that it is approximately real-time.

An interlaced monitor running inside the frames or scenes of the movie will have to be running slower. Now, we won't see the frame breaks unless we use our peripheral vision, but you will almost see the breaks, which in itself creates the effect of the monitor screen flickering. Flickering is directly attributable to the monitor being interlaced.

Non-interlaced techniques eliminate this frame-breaking. As such, the display image is a continuous rolling display. The display image is still a compilation of many frames in many applications, but the computer user does not see this. And the monitor does not flicker.

Whatever may be actively residing in memory and concurrently being displayed on the monitor screen can also be directed as output to a printer, though formatting of the output becomes a major consideration. This is because there are other features and functions provided by the application software, which can affect your output.

Printer function is more complicated, because there are more things that can go wrong when printing. A monitor device is pretty much hardware dependent. The monitor, regardless of size and type, gets plugged into the video port, which is connected to the main Data BUS on the computer.

There are a limited number of options which the user can set via buttons or knobs on the monitor itself. Most folks just 'plug and go'. That is, they accept the default settings and use the monitor as is.

On the other hand, there are software selectable options through the operating system software that can be adjusted to change some of the display options. This is typically done through the display setting function of the OS. This would include options for 'Wallpaper' or 'Background' to be displayed on the screen when the computer is on, but the user is not running any applications. Or, the user may have one or more applications running but have them 'minimized'. (Minimized is a 'WINDOWS' term that means that the application is active but not visible on the display screen.)

Also, 'screen-saver' settings are another popular user-selectable option for the monitor. This is a feature that brings up for display a unique selectable image, when the computer detects that there is no activity on the system. The computer infers no activity when there have been no keyboard strokes, or mouse movements, completed over a predetermined number of seconds. Usually the seconds set ranges between 1 and 300 or, up to 5 minutes.

Screen-savers have become very popular in the work environment for two reasons. One is that the user can load a screen-saver of choice. For example, the one I truly enjoy is the Aquarium screen-saver where a simulated ocean life with fish actually swimming can be seen. When it kicks in, one can see fish come to life on the screen. Customized screen savers have been found to be appealing to the eye. Some folks have photographs of their favorite people digitized into BYTE-sized files. They then load the files containing the digitized version (or, you could say, the 'BIT-form') of the photograph(s)into their screen- saver function for use as a screen saver or as wallpaper.

Another reason screen-savers have become popular is that they provide some degree of security. They do this by obscuring what is on the screen when you are not using the computer but want to keep whatever it is you are working on up on the screen. Furthermore, if you put a password on your screen saver then upon returning to use the computer, you are prompted for the password immediately after pressing any key. A would-be saboteur waiting to gain access to your computer would be thwarted from gaining access to your computer in your absence, because they won't presumably know your password.

Printers

If you can see it on the screen display you can usually print it out on a printer. I say usually, because to a large extent, what you can print out is determined by the software you have installed to support printing. Like the monitor that uses video driver programs to manipulate color in screen output, printers require driver program software to manipulate printer or 'hardcopy' output.

Printing is more of a challenge to the average computer user because more things can go wrong with printing than with screen display output. Once a copy of the desired BYTE size file exits the main Data BUS on its way to the printer, a certain amount of control also leaves the main Data BUS with the file copy.

And at that point in time, what determines whether or not you get the hardcopy output desired will be your pre-configured printer set up. If the print options are set optimally through your software on the computer, quality output is assured. Another factor is the configuration of the printing device to communicate with the BYTE size file(s)you will be sending to the printer. So, the printer needs to be set up, on the computer, and on the printer itself.

Monitors are largely hardware-dependent and default driven. Plug it in to the video connection port, and it pretty much functions as designed. Some additional features can be obtained with the video software.

However, printers need to be set up. The settings can and will need to be reset depending on how you want to format your output for each 'job' you want to print in hardcopy format at the time of printing. Important considerations when printing are type of hardcopy, size of paper-whether it be standard 8 1/2 by 11" or legal size-and whether you will be printing on special forms or envelopes. Portrait versus landscape has become a popular setting change when printing. Portrait size is regular 8 1/2 by 11", and landscape being 11 by 8 1/2".

Printing technology has come a long way in the last few years. And the procedures for printing have become largely standardized across many types of printers. As such it becomes important to ask what differentiates printers? And it comes down to 5 important things.

First and foremost is the type of printer technology used to support printing. By far the leader in this class would be laser printers. Their quality and speed has gone up and their cost continues to come down. Impact printers continue to be sold and used, even though this printer technology is slowly fading out of this current computer generation. Impact printers in all likelihood, will not be used in future generations of printers.

Second, printers can be differentiated on size, which includes 2 size categories: The physical size of the printer, and the physical size of the output it can produce. Large specialty printers used for printing all sizes and types of printed output like wall charts, building blueprints and the like are in a class of their own. More typically today, we have printers used for output sizes handling at a minimum 8.5" by 11" and 11" by 14" paper, as well as standard envelopes. The physical size of these printers is approximately desktop or table size. This size of printer today accommodates the largest percentage of computer printers used for commercial and consumer applications.

Third, printers are distinguished between color output capability or no color. Color laser printers are more expensive as quality and size of output increases. Also, cost of maintenance for color printers is generally more expensive, because one has to buy and insert, as needed, the more expensive color toner containers (i.e. bottles or cartridges).

Dusting and cleaning are absolutely necessary for satisfactory results. Make sure you consult your owner's manual. Color printers are generally slower than non-color when speed is held as a constant. This is because color output needs more time to process. I tell my students that color output needs more time to cook in the oven before it is ready. Non-color printers are generally cheaper and faster when all variables are held constant. But if you need color output, non-color is not an option. Until the color printer technology becomes perfected, I recommend that if you need color, buy a good quality color laser printer, because the lower-end color printers currently available are really not capable of turning out the quality of output you might need.

That is to say, that the cost to maintain low-end color printers is not, in my opinion, justifiable.

Fourth, we can differentiate printers between the categories of a stand-alone or slave printer, and printers which have become known as "shared", meaning, the printer is on a Network, and print output can be sent to the shared printer by more than one person. These two types of printers are also referred to as 'local' and 'networked printers', respectively.

The distinction is somewhat obvious, and many intuitive cost factors enter into the picture. Stand-alone printers basically connect into the PC via a parallel interface. Serial interfaces are still used for slave printers, but you need to understand that with serial, the printer will process slower. This is because a serial interface connected into the main Data BUS will enable BITs which make up the BYTEs to go out to the slave printer one BIT at a time. Parallel printer interfaces send out one or more BYTEs at a time depending on what size Data BUS and what size parallel interface we are working with. The point is, that more BITs off the Data BUS are transferred in the same time period with parallel transfer.

Network, or shared printers have become much more common since the early 90's. Their cost generally has and continues to come down while their speed and quality has gone up. The big cost savings are coming from the proliferation of networks in organizations everywhere. Given a network in place, it makes better cost sense to get a high-capacity, high-quality printer on the network and let many users send output to it versus getting individual printers for everyone who needs to print output.

Lastly, even if we no longer used older impact printing technology, we need to differentiate printers according to speed. Printer speed is measured using three important factors. First is the number of pages that can be printed per minute. The abbreviation is ppm. Second is the number of lines per minute. This is abbreviated as lpm. Lpm is not used that much anymore with the overwhelming proliferation of laser printers. However with impact printers, lpm was a major criterion. Indeed the larger impact printers used to be categorized as line printers. And the third factor is characters per second, abbreviated as cps.

For the purposes of measuring and evaluating printers you can think of cps equalling BYTEs per second. However don't confuse with bps (BITs-per-second) And if you are not into any esoteric mathematical applications, cps is a good printer assessment criterion. In other words, the higher the cps rating, the faster the printer.

When printing, ppm (pages per minute)is perhaps the most important factor. Imagine, if you will, printing out a report that contains, say, 50 letter-size pages. If you had your choice, would you prefer a printer that can pump it out at 8 pages per minute, or a printer that can process output at 28 pages per minute? This may seem like a big difference, but imagine yourself waiting for your output after having sent it to the printer, especially if it is a shared printer. Shared or networked printing means there will be other people's print jobs sent to this same printer. The 8 ppm printer will take 6-7 minutes. The 28 ppm printer will take 1-2 minutes. This is after the printer starts your print job on a shared printer.

Now, if a particular person does a substantial amount of printing, and time is of the essence, then generally the solution is to give that person his/her own dedicated printer ('dedicated' refers to any device that is used for whatever reason by only one person or station). Sometimes also referred to as "stand-alone". Or simply, 'local'.

11

BYTE Summary

The BYTE is the mechanism by which the computer and computer network are able to assign or derive meaning from all that it processes and stores over time. You need to know the BYTE, because BYTE management determines to what extent you can guide your company, your students, your family and yourself in managing computer-related resources.

The BYTE is what leads us into the higher levels of computer and computer networking. That is, where we humans derive value and meaning from the underlying supportive technology of the computer, which is inherently binary and driven by the BIT.

The BYTE is where we find meaning in all that the computer networks can process. Meaning is derived from the 2 distinct type of BYTEs. These 2 types are mathematical and nonmathematical BYTEs. Understanding this important distinction is key to managing your memory and storage capacities and for knowing to what extent your staff; coworkers or your students need computer resources.

Processing mathematical compared to nonmathematical BYTEs presents different operational criteria which impacts your computer system in different ways. Mathematical BYTEs have a variable BYTE capacity, whereas non-mathematical BYTEs are largely predetermined and predictable. Knowing the BYTE means knowing this important distinction.

Mathematical BYTEs can vary in size. Non-mathematical BYTEs are predefined in terms of how many BITs per BYTE, the precise number of BITs per BYTE is based on the standardized character code being used on the particular computer. Each type of BYTE will have varying memory and storage requirements. Mathematical BYTE unit memory and BYTE storage requirements vary according to the size and type of calculations being processed. BYTEs which equal a letter, a nonmathematical number, or a special character, have predefined BYTE unit memory and BYTE storage requirements.

Memory is one of the major power factors of any computer. The more memory you have on-board the more you can do, and the faster you can do it. The BYTE is the single-most important characteristic of memory, and for that matter, secondary storage.

Memory chips are a string or sequence of storage units. The power, or the magic, becomes evident when you consider: the computer can store BYTEs in these chips at nearly the speed of light, remember the order or sequence in which it did the storing, calculate an address location for each and every BYTE unit of memory storage and retrieve any and all BYTE units currently stored in memory.

One salient feature of all BYTEs is to recognize that we human users of the computer, and the computer network, derive meaning or subjective value from the computer's output through the great quantities of BYTEs which get displayed for us across the screen, printed for us on hardcopy output and which are stored permanently for us on secondary storage. It helps facilitate better comprehension of the BYTE, if you know its underlying origins.

If you do not understand the BYTE, you cannot comprehend the extent to which your coworker, support staff, students or children can utilize their computer resources. You also will not realize when they make requests to extend or expand the resources that they have, what they actually are trying to do. Hard disk capacity upgrades will have a more realistic meaning for you if you know the BYTE. I always say "the more you give them that works, the more they want to work with it". This means that if computer usage goes well, you can expect it to grow. You need to know the BYTE to be able to support your folks growing with their computer resources.

You need to know the BYTE in order to understand how memory gets loaded. Memory is measured and managed in BYTEs. BYTEs take up residence for the life of the current computer session in addressable units of storage. It is useful to consider that a single BYTE of information, say a letter, number, or a special character, will require exactly one unit of storage in main memory to be active. Understanding this process enables you to support your computer users more effectively.

Thinking about the BYTE in terms of being a single character of information helps to understand how many BYTEs are typically needed to create or open a meaningful file of BYTEs. Or to use a software package which is made up of one or more files of BYTEs. Since everything has to be loaded into memory to become usable, the road to meaningful information being displayed on your monitor, output to your printer, or transferred over your computer network is through BYTE unit addressable memory. If the information you seek cannot be loaded in BYTE form into your computer's memory, you will not be able to get what you seek. Knowing the BYTE means knowing this important element.

To summarize, we need to know that the BYTE is the major element necessary for us users to understand how it is possible for the computer to process and deliver meaningful information, both on the monitor display and through hardcopy printed output.

- You need to know the BYTE to comprehend how information is processed through memory. That is, main memory, or RAM. The more capacity for storing BYTEs in memory, the more power your computer will have in terms of how much it can process at any given time, and how fast it can process. Knowing the BYTE means you can manage and measure your memory capacity. And knowing this enables you to be more supportive of the folks that use the computer resources.

- You need to know BYTE to understand how information is processed, saved and retrieved from secondary storage. Specifically, hard disk, diskette, CD-ROM and the forthcoming writable CDs. Like main memory, management and measurement of BYTE capacities become important computer user tasks. Knowing the BYTE means you can save and retrieve BYTE-filled files of information on selected secondary storage devices such as the hard disk. And that you can selectively choose at the time of saving or retrieval which secondary storage device to utilize among those that you have connected to your computer's main Data BUS.

- You need to know the BYTE because it is at the core of the Year 2000 (Y2K) set of problems. That is, the Y2K set problems is primarily a BYTE problem. How can we continue to express the year using only the last two digits of the year, which is to say 2 BYTEs for the year, in the year 2000? Obviously the year 00 does not convey the essential meaning of the year 2000, as does 98 or 99 for 1998 and 1999 respectively. In Part IV I detail the Y2K set of problems. But, fundamentally Y2K is a BIT and a BYTE Problem. It's BYTEs that process in embedded system chips. It's BYTEs that transmit through processor and network hardware. Lastly, it's BYTEs that are programmed in all of the software known to man, both systems software, and applications software. Including all existing software and all software yet to be developed up through and beyond the year 2000.

• Moreover this Y2K dilemma will have an acute impact on computer applications where the date field is used in calculations. (that would be in applications processing the year digits as <u>mathematical</u> BYTEs) Things like dividends, finance charges and interest payments, just to name a few problem areas, will be affected by Y2K. The cure for this problem is in making the computer and computer network capable of supporting and processing applications that express the date field using 4 mathematical BYTEs, rather than 2 mathematical BYTEs. Or, at least being able to transmit a 2-BYTE year and subsequently through the software, process it as its correct year (i.e. 2000, 2001, etc.) Knowing the BYTE enables you to be more effective in responding to this problem and any related issues.

• Lastly, you need to know BYTE, in particular, how the BYTE is organized with other BYTEs to construct larger BYTE containers which are files of BYTEs, or simply files. The computer and the computer network both are "file-driven". On the computer, a variable number of BITs make up a mathematical, and/or, a non-mathematical BYTE. A variable number of BYTEs make up a file. Building on this BIT-to-BYTE to file principle, we turn now to Part III, the computer network, where a similar principle operates. BITs process into BYTEs, which, like the larger file, are processed into a new type of container. This container's type depends on the 'transport' service being used to network. Our transport choices are numerous. An example of a transport would be "frame-relay". This transport uses a container referred to as a 'Packet'. The packet like most of the transport containers can hold huge quantities of BITs and BYTEs, which get processed, then transferred over the network. Modem methods excepted, transfers usually occur at high rates of speed over such networks. The prevalent network transport services are summarized in Part III.

PART III
the Network

12

Why Do I Need to Know the Network?

Perhaps the hottest of areas in the Year 1998, relevant to the computer, is computer networking, or Telecommunications. The only other hotter topic I can think of would be the integration of computer networking with traditional telephone, and now video-conferencing capabilities. These are reasons enough to want to know more about networking. But I can give you a few more.

Y2K is not far away. The network is a critical component in any organization's infrastructure, and will need to play a vital role in the coming Y2K confusion. The main reason is that even if your organization does an impeccable job of getting Y2K compliant, massive and costly problems can still happen from the interconnections with company's that are not Y2K compliant.

The buck needs to stop at the network. This is where you put in place safeguards against non-compliant data getting into your network and causing problems.

Just in the past year we have had huge mergers among the Telecommunications giants. AT & T with TCI and TCG. MCI with Worldcomm. NORTEL with Bay Networks. QUEST with LCI. This means intensified competition. Knowing the network, the network marketplace.

And how providers like AT & T and the rest price out their services, will enable you to optimize your available resources and the additional services that you may need to acquire. Knowing how these services are priced out is invaluable. Good network design fundamentals can save your organization a great deal of money. I know, I have done it many times over.

Many other reasons exist for knowing network principles. However we will be going beyond the scope of this book if we stray to far from the BIT, and the BYTE.

The scope of this book precludes much detail on voice and video, but I hope you will gain a strong sense of how, for the most part, the industry prices out all three network media's (data, voice, video) through my discussion of bandwidth. Essentially, like computer data voice and video signals become 'BITs' in order to be transmitted. You need to know bandwidth, because it is at the core of knowing any type of network.

You need to know how BITs & BYTEs relate to networking because every home and building, for the most part, will eventually be connected. In fact, at this time, some estimates are predicting that there will be 200 million Internet users by the year 2000. This means that 200 million people with computers, either in their homes, or at the corporate office, with either a modem or much higher speed interface will have the ability to traverse time and distance in communicating with anyone else on the Internet at a global level.

Even small companies, if doing any business at all, will in some way get networked, even if it is just a low-end dial-up PC connection to the Internet and the World Wide WEB. Or, if it is a larger corporation, with multiple sites running integrated data, voice and video over the same transport infrastructure.

Knowing how BITs & BYTEs relate to the network will sharpen your perspective on the Y2K set of problems. Afterall, the Y2K set of problems is in its inception, a BYTE-storage problem. However, the Y2K problem set has only expanded with the evolution of software and hardware. In its infancy, it was a BYTE storage problem. BYTE problems are BIT problems. BIT problems become network problems.

On the surface, the fix is simple. Use 4 BYTEs to express the year for 2000 and up through 9999. However, after five decades of using a 2-BYTE year in application programs and in transmitting 2-BYTE year fields over the technically evolving networks, we have created a problematic situation that cannot be resolved that simply. Hardware for the computer and the computer network must be made to be Y2K compliant. All of the software that has been programmed to process the year as a 2-BYTE field, must be modified or replaced to be Y2K compliant.

You need to know how BITs & BYTEs relate to the network, because there are cost economies associated with the various types of network transport infrastructures supporting telecommunications. Knowing BITs & BYTEs prepares you to meet this networking challenge.

If you can integrate the BITs & BYTEs which support transfer of data, voice and video over the same transport, you can save yourself and/or your company a lot of money. This is where the technology is going these days.

In Part II we covered Files. BITs & BYTEs make up all file types. And everything moves in files on the Computer. But on the Network, Files coming off of the computer BUS are reorganized prior to transmission. I like to say files get "sliced and diced" at the BIT level prior to network transmission. Actually, the files get repackaged into a different kind of container.

Depending on the network type and the network protocols, these containers can be called simply a "BIT Stream". In the case of the modem type of transmission where you basically send 1 ASCII BYTE, which is 7 BITs, plus 1 start, 1 parity and 1 stop BIT, this means a total of 10 BITs for each BYTE being transmitted. So when using the modem type of transport, figure generally that 70% of the transmission will be actual payload information. In this example, the information would be the sum total of all of the 7-BIT BYTEs contained in each "BIT Stream" which are included in the file to be transferred. The other 30% is the 'overhead' BITs which are required to support the transmission of the payload. Each BYTE in the file would go out or be received in this way, until the whole file is transmitted.

Other larger capacity networks use packets, frames, blocks or envelopes. And each of these methods has a different overhead-to-payload ratio. The specific way in which BITs and BYTEs are repackaged to be networked is a direct function of the network transport type and the protocols operating on the network being used.

You need to know about BITs & BYTEs networking because just as the mailing of a letter requires some overhead costs, like postage, envelopes, etc. to transmit the information content you place in the envelope, computer networking requires some varying amount of 'overhead BITs' with every transmission. The amount of overhead BITs is directly related to the type of networking technology being used.

Bandwidth, measured in BITs-per-second, is one essential element that network service providers use to assess the recurring charges to its customers. Bandwidth is how big a 'pipe' you have for supporting network transmission. By 'pipe' I mean the total number of BITs you can transmit in any given second. That is how network bandwidth is measured. The term 'pipe' is a 'shop talk' term that we use in the industry. (i.e. big pipes can transmit more BITs than small pipes).

As such, bandwidth is directly related to dollars. And, it relates directly to network performance. More bps means, presumably, better performance. Having a BIT & BYTE sense of networking will make you more effective when it comes to managing computer network resources and guiding your folks in their pursuit of 'best approaches' to the computer network.

Knowing BITs & BYTEs as they relate to networking will help you understand the various network technologies which I summarize in Chapter 14 under the heading of Prevalent Network Transports. Being familiar with this network Transport List from a BIT & BYTE perspective makes you more competent to respond to network technology decision transactions. But before we go there I want to further embellish this whole notion of transporting (hence 'Network Transport') BITs & BYTEs.

13

Transporting Information BYTEs and Overhead BITs

With the inception of modems into the world of the computer, a whole new definition of the BIT began to evolve. It continues to evolve today. The modem enabled us to not only view electrical current as signal voltage but also as signal voltage that could be transferred over long distances using the Telephone Cabling system already in place. Indeed, this cabling system itself is growing and evolving in support of voice communications.

In Part I, I discussed the modem as a serial device which transfers BITs over the phone lines as "HIGH" or "LOW" pulses. The modem has evolved in many ways since its inception, but like the computer, continues to operate on its original basic principle. And that is to convert the signals coming out of the computer's Data BUS into "HIGH" or "LOW" pulses. The technical term for this conversion is known as Modulation. And at the remote end the corresponding modem reconverts the "HIGH" or "LOW" pulses back to original form prior to inputting the signals onto the remote computer's Data BUS. The reconversion is known as Demodulation.

The modem derives its name from the 2 conversion processes. The MO in modem comes from MOdulation. The DEM comes from DEModulation. And since the modem's birth it has gone through numerous changes, upgrades, revisions, standards. It is also a good example of the SCFB Paradox I discussed in Part I. Because it truly has gotten smaller, cheaper, faster and better.

The early modems were very expensive. Nowadays most PCs come with a built-in modem. You might have to make a special order to not get the modem. And if you did, you would only save about $50. But watch your shipping charges, because you might end up paying more than if you simply took the computer system with the modem.

The networking of computers began in the early days with the deployment of modems. Networking is the name which evolved to describe the connecting of 2 or more computers.

Today we have numerous other forms of networking to consider. Though slow compared to today's standards, networking through modems in the early-modem days then was referred to as "High Speed Networking". The first operational modems ran at 300BAUD, or 300 BITs-per-second. And it was typical to connect only 2 computers-one local and one at the remote end. The concept here became known as a point-to-point network.

Today's latest consumer standard modem on the market operates at 56Kbps. That is, 56,000 BITs-per-second. In using modems today, we have numerous computers connecting to numerous other computers. Point-to-point networking is still applied, but many other forms of networking computers have been developed.

Network Transport Required

The form which the computer network takes today is called the Network Transport. When we use a modem-type connection to network, this is referred to as any of the following: dialup network access or simply dialup, asynchronous, local switched access, or simply, remote dial access. (Dial access today is the low end and the slow end for an individual to connect to a computer network.) Perhaps the most common term for it today is simply 'dial access', even though we no longer use dialers, we just key in the phone number via the keyboard.

You may surmise from the above that there are already phone lines all over the place to support voice and/or modem types of connections. You would be correct. Furthermore, the number of circuits is growing rapidly. Indeed, as we read here, the local phone companies all over the country are creating new area codes to assign to areas which used to be considered a local calling area. This means that in the effected areas, people will have to start using an additional 4 numbers to make what used to be only a 7-digit call. And this same number of digits required in establishing the connection would apply equally as well for voice and/or modem connections.

All of the existing circuit switched lines in the country constitute what I call our country's infrastructure for 'public circuit switched access'. Using this infrastructure for dial access is cheap, because its primary purpose is to support voice traffic. And it already exists. No one has to design and build a new network transport infrastructure if you want to network via modem. You simply use your existing phone line or order the startup-connection of a new line from the enumeral existing lines owned by the local phone company.

And you pay whatever applicable charges would apply as if you were making a phone call. If the computer or computer network you are dialing into is local, you pay whatever you would pay for a local call. If the computer or computer network is far away, you would pay the equivalent recurring charges as you would for a toll call. In this case, as with any toll call, time becomes a critical cost factor.

As you can see, the modem illustrates for us a method of computer networking via the public switched transport infrastructure. Computer networking today takes place over many different types of infrastructure transports. Computer networking, from the slowest of the slow modems, to the ultra high-speed networks of current day, require an infrastructure transport. That is, they require an underlying, physical, method of connection. Modem-type network connections are a good example of using the public switched transport infrastructure.

In Part I, we compared the computer's main Data BUS to a highway. The computer network transport is like the principal highway that connects the many, varied and lessor main data BUSes (i.e. video BUS, address BUS) of the individual computers which are connected to the network. In Part III, will summarize the other prevalent network transports. But before I do this I need to continue my abuse of the modem in illustrating a few other principal elements of computer networking.

Networking Costs

The next element we need to understand is that all methods of networking have a cost. This cost relates back to overall bandwidth, or BITs-per-second, capacity of the network. Generally, more bps means more cost in dollars. Therefore, it comes down to what in BIT terms is going across the network. And what goes across is a combination of the information or data you need to transfer, and a variable amount of 'overhead' BITs, which are needed to support the actual transfer.

When you mail a letter you have overhead associated with the envelope, the postage stamp, the need to address and write a return address on the envelope and the cost of the envelope itself. This is in addition to the content that you enclose inside the envelope. Also, you have a choice of methods for mailing the letter. First class, overnight, return receipt required, etc.

Similarly, the various types of computer networking have a varying degree of BIT overhead associated with them. And the modem is once again a good networking method to illustrate in principal form networking BIT overhead.

Earlier I stated that modems were characterized by "BAUD" rate, or simply BITs-per-second.

We no longer use the BAUD rate designator. This is because the standards governing modem BIT transmissions have evolved such that 1 BAUD now consistently equals 1 BIT. In the early days, 1 BAUD could have meant more than 1 BIT. It is technical, so I won't go there. But suffice it to say that modems today are characterized by their respective BITs-per-second rate.

Now, more frequently, we are seeing and hearing the modem referred to as a 28.8K or a 56K modem. What is meant with the K designator is Kilo-BITs-Per-Second.

When 1200BAUD modems came out, they were heralded as the device of the century. It was the modem that quadrupled the speed of what, then, was considered "High Speed Networking".

Given where we are today with networking and where we were when we got started, it is useful and relevant to the topic of networking for you to understand how the BIT and BYTE evolved relative to the early modems.

Earlier in Part I, I used the example of modem to illustrate how a serial interface to the main Data BUS works. Each BYTE coming out of the computer BUS, whether it be a mathematical BYTE or a nonmathematical BYTE, goes through the modem on its way out to the network. In the modem the BYTEs get converted through modulation into a series of "HIGH" and "LOW" pulses that are the corresponding equivalent to the same binary form of each BYTE which existed on the computer's BUS prior to its going into the modem.

Now, before the modem can modulate the BYTE over the network, the modem has to add a few BITs so that it can first of all mark the beginning and end of the BYTE. Obviously, if the modem is going to send huge quantities of BYTEs over this network to a remote computer, within the signal transmission of it all there needs to be a way to mark the beginning of each BYTE and the end of each BYTE. In this way the remote computer can differentiate among all of the BYTEs in the transmission that it will receive from the sending computer.

Lets say you are sending a file which contains 5KB or 5,000 BYTEs of non-mathematical information. The modem needs to be able to mark the beginning and end of each of the 5,000 BYTEs in this transmission. The way the modem accommodates this need is to place a start BIT at the beginning of each BYTE, and a stop BIT at the end of each BYTE. The Start and Stop BITs are HIGH BITs, represented with a 1.

In addition, to make sure the BYTE gets transmitted correctly the modem employs a technique known as Parity Checking. When used, Parity checking adds yet one more BIT to each BYTE of transmission over the modem network. Parity checking comes in three modes; EVEN, ODD and NONE. If Parity is set to EVEN, then each BYTE is immediately followed in transmission by either a HIGH or a LOW pulse, which indicates that the sum of the HIGH BITs that make up this BYTE are an even number. Like 2,4,6 or 8. The reverse is true for the option of ODD parity. If parity option is NONE then there is no parity BIT.

The point of all this detail on modem BYTE transmission is that the modem network process adds a degree of BIT overhead to the actual transmission. This overhead adds to the size and throughput requirements for the overall BIT transmission. Transmitting a single ASCII non-mathematical BYTE, for example, is not just 7 BITs, which is what an ASCII BYTE would normally be.

In order to transmit 7 BITs using a modem, we need a Start, a Stop, and maybe an optional Parity BIT. This makes the total transmission per BYTE equal to 10 BITs with a Parity BIT. If it were an EBCDIC BYTE we would add the same 3 overhead BITs to an 8 BIT BYTE for a total of 11 BITs per BYTE transmission, and so on.

This form of sending and receiving BYTEs is referred to technically as Asynchronous Transmission. What this means is that each BYTE follows a process which begins with a Start BIT and ends with a Stop BIT. It is also called Start-Stop Transmission. The Start-Stop functions add overhead BITs to the overall transmission.

Understand that any form of computer networking adds overhead BITs to the transmission of meaningful BYTEs of information. The extent to which overhead BITs are added is a major principal factor in evaluating the cost of computer networking.

Modems are a good beginning point in discussing the networking of BYTEs, because it can be readily shown at the BIT level how overhead gets added to each and every single BYTE being transmitted. Since BYTEs, and the files made up of BYTEs, are what contain the meaningful information in any transmission, it is useful to know the BIT overhead of networking that is meaningful or important, versus that which is only needed to support the transmission of it all.

All forms of computer networking have BIT overhead. In computer networking with the modem as our first example, there is some BIT overhead associated with the actual transport of each and every BYTE, and thus any and all files included in the process. This BIT overhead is essential to completing network transmission. It is a vital characteristic in designing and costing out computer-based networks.

BIT overhead exists with all forms of networking. Thus it is an important consideration in estimating the cost and timing of networking. BIT & BYTE economies of time, speed and size necessarily apply. It becomes an even larger matter of importance as the size and speed requirements of the network grows. Users, though largely unable to technically explain it, want and need more BITs-per-second for less dollars.

This is the core of what I call the "Bandwidth Dilemma". More BITs-per-second equals more bandwidth. More bandwidth means scaling up the network transport. More bandwidth means greater speeds are obtainable, more end-users can be networked and greater volumes of BIT traffic are possible.

Bandwidth requirements determine the size & type of network transport. The major factor in costing out networks is bandwidth, or BITs-per-second capacity. How many BITs can be transferred per second? And more importantly, we need to know how many of the BITs with each transmission are overhead BITs, compared to how many BITs in a given network transmission are used in defining actual BYTEs or meaningful information.

The types, sizes and corresponding costs of networks, expressed in BIT overhead, as well as other overhead costs, have increased dramatically since the early modem days. And the processes used to network have also adapted to a networking environment that has demanded of itself to become-to a large extent—mobile. That is to say, have the computer network resources available whenever, wherever needed. Whether it be through a cell phone modem, regular phone system modem, satellite up/down link, or private or public network connection.

You may have heard the saying "time is money". The whole domain of modern day telecommunications brings this anthem to life like no other technology. Because of the tremendous power and speed capacities now available in support of networking, and because the network transport is unemotional, it doesn't care if your BITs are overhead BITs, or if your BITs formulate meaningful BYTEs. The total time it takes and the total BITs that you send/receive over the network will, in one form or another, come back to you in the form of dollar costs. And for situations where more than a simple dial access is needed, the greater part of the networking costs, for example, in companies having multiple sites to connect regionally, nationally or even globally, is going to be in the recurring charges (usually monthly) associated with providing the network transport.

14

Network Transports Support Network Processes

I stated earlier that the form that the computer network takes today is called the network transport. I described the modem type of network connection as simply dialup access. I described what I call the infrastructure for supporting dialup networking. Using this infrastructure for dial access is cheap, because its primary purpose is to support voice traffic. It already exists. And it is growing daily. Ten years ago it was rare when a home had more than one phone line. Today it is more common to have at least two phone lines in the same home.

No one has to design and build a new network transport infrastructure for you if you want to network via modem. You can simply use your existing phone line or order a new line from the phone company if you need a line dedicated for this purpose. Remember, any voice line can be used to support a modem connection. Wherever you can modulate voice signals, you can modulate data signals.

The modem method of computer networking typically implies,

again, the use of what is called the public switched transport infrastructure. Computer networking today takes place over many different types of infrastructure transports. However I want to emphasize here that any type of computer networking requires a transport infrastructure, from the slowest and cheapest modem type connections which make use of the public switched transport on up to the superfast Asynchronous Transfer Mode (ATM) type transport which operate at bandwidth speeds up to 155Mbps and the SONET OC-12 at 622Mbps, as well as OC-48 and other transports which operate in excess of these BIT thresholds.

The computer network transport is to the network what the computer main Data BUS is to the individual computer. There are numerous types of computer network transports operating today. Some in the public sector, others in the private sector. A large percentage of these transports, except for wireless and satellite types of transports use pre-existing phone line or phone line conduits to optimize, install or lay in the necessary cabling. It is easy to see how today's computer network transports followed closely, at least in terms of installation around the country, the transports installed that support phone or voice communications.

Network Transport Summary

I began this chapter with reference again to the modem type of connection, because I know that many users out there have at least heard of modem. And most computers sold today come with a modem. However as you can see with the following table, there are several other networking technology transport services available these days. Perhaps the major distinction among these is that only a few are available in the home. However, this will change.

Prevalent Network Transports

Transport	Bandwidth*	Media Type	Base Use	Cost Method	Comments
MODEM	56 Kbps	phone lines	Home Office	recurring time	works but slow
ISDN	128 Kbps	phone lines	Home Office	recurring time	data, voice video
ADSL	1.5 Mbps	phone lines	Home Office	monthly	still problems
Frame relay	1.5 Mbps	copper or fiber	Corporate	monthly	must lease
T-1	1.5 Mbps	copper or fiber	Corporate	monthly	must lease
Cable MODEM	10 Mbps	cable lines	Home	monthly	Coming soon
Ethernet	10 Mbps	copper fiber	Corporate	start-up only	company owned
Token-ring	16 Mbps	copper or fiber	Corporate	start-up only	company owned
DS-3	45 Mbps	copper or fiber	Corporate	monthly	must lease
Satellite	64 Mbps	wireless	Corporate	monthly	must lease
Fast Ethernet	100 Mbps	copper or fiber	Corporate	start-up only	company owned
FDDI	100 Mbps	fiber	Corporate	start-up only	company owned
ATM	155 Mbps	copper or fiber	Corporate	monthly	must lease
OC-3	155 Mbps	fiber-optic	Corporate	monthly	must lease
OC-12	622 Mbps	fiber-optic	Corporate	monthly	must lease
GigaBIT LAN	1.0 Gbps	copper or fiber	Corporate	start-up only	company owned

*maximum bandwidth listed

Network Transport Means Network Process & Procedures

A principal worth noting about computer network transports is that transports support process(es). In the case of computer networking, every transport type has one or more corresponding process(es) for connecting and operating over the network. The modem, once again in its simplicity, will serve further to illustrate the network transport process.

Assuming the computer has the hardware and software installed to network via modem, and the computer's modem is plugged into both computer and the phone line, we start by clicking on the modem icon. Software is loaded, and the computer, via modem, dials the destination modem via the public circuit switched network transport. Once connected to the destination modem, a link between the destination modem and the host, or destination computer, is established.

To get connected, once the remote (end user) modem places the call out over the phone line, the call must go to the remote users phone switching center usually located within a few miles from the remote user's home. Once the call reaches this switching center, the call is redirected to the regional switching center. Here the call is switched out to the individual line, (usually the last 4 digits of the phone number) or the line which connects the destination computer's modem.

If the destination modem and computer's phone number has an area code, an additional switching center would be involved in call setup. Once connected, there exists for the length of the call, a temporary circuit between the remote user's computer and the host destination computer.

This is the same process that a voice call would go through, except that there would be no modems, and the two end computers would be manned by people using telephones, not computers. And in the case of a phone number which has an area code, (i.e. long distance) an additional switching center would also be in the loop in order to complete the process.

Network transports and process goes hand in hand. Some transports utilize many processes in support of multiple applications. At a remote end, a company might have localized transports in place to carry computer connections, voice (phone) and videoconferencing. Each of the three may come into a local private facility where the three types of signals are processed out over a singular high bandwidth backbone transport. That transport carries all three signals at approximately the same time to the destination site where the three types of signals are broken out. They are then carried into the respective destination devices (i.e. computer, phone and video screen) for use by the people at the other end.

A great place to start in becoming familiar with your computer network, whatever transport you have in place to work with, is try to find out what process(es) your transport supports. Wherever you have a network process you will have a physical transport. And wherever you have a physical transport you will have one or more network processes.

The demand for more bandwidth will be met by the increasing deployment of network transport services by the network provider companies. At the local levels, that is, metropolitan areas where the descendants of the Regional Bell Operating companies tend to dominate the network transport services marketplace, there is a convergence of network technologies. It is fueled by passage of 1996's Telecomm Act. This is the law that enabled long distance providers to compete for local service customers, and has led to local service companies competing for long-distance service customers.

15

Protocols & Vehicles: Rules of the Networking Road

The modem gave way to many and numerous forms of networking technology. So much so that we had virtual chaos in the world of networking up through the mid-80s. Many manufacturers were putting out different forms of their recommended approaches to networking, some improving on the modem, others being touted as the "new generation" of networking. All, in some way or another, proffering their respective method of computer networking.

Standards to the Rescue

Because of the large amount of variation in computer networking products, incompatibilities existed everywhere. The good news is that the standards which have been following behind the manufacture of the computer itself these past 50 years have caught up with the world of networks & telecommunications. Manufacturers began to form standards committees on specific computer and computer network technologies.

The U. S. government got involved in computer network-related standards with the promulgation of the International Standards Organization's Open Systems Interconnect (OSI) networking model. The government created a regulation which simply said that to do business with the U.S. government on all computer and computer network related transactions, the hardware and software involved had to be OSI compliant. What OSI compliance, or as we say 'Open' means is that if a specific hardware and software item is 'Open', it is compliant with the standard protocols defined in the OSI Model.

The International Standards Organization (ISO) takes credit for coordinating the development of the OSI model. You might be asking yourself, 'What is a Model?'. Many of my students over the years have asked that question every time I discuss the topic of computer network models. Think of a model along the lines of a model airplane kit. Not quite out of my favorite movie, 'Babes In Toyland', but surely it takes us back a few years.

The model airplane kit comes with a set of specifications on how to build the airplane model. Usually if we follow the specifications, glue and snap everything in place according to directions, we end up with a smaller scale model of the "real thing" airplane.

A computer network model is a set of specifications which provides the directions and specifies the rules for building a computer network. The OSI model is an open systems model. We understand open to be a term which represents 'Open' to any manufacturer's computer hardware and software. OSI uses a layered approach to specifying what hardware and software is required in order to connect up a network, and to connect devices such as computers to that network. The OSI model is quite abstract and beyond the scope of this book. But suffice it to say that if the hardware and/or the software you may be considering for your network design is OSI compliant, than you have met the first great challenge in designing your network.

The OSI model contrasts sharply with a few other computer network models. IBM developed their own, called the Systems Network Application (SNA) computer network model. Also DEC developed the DECnet or Digital Equipment Network model. Both SNA and DECnet are proprietary models. That is, these two models are based on hardware and software that are strictly manufactured by IBM and DEC respectively.

Needless to say, since the inception in the mid-80s of all 3 network models: OSI, SNA and DECnet, much has happened in terms of smaller, cheaper, faster and presumably better technology. PCs and related technology used in client-server environments have taken away a large part of the market share for computer network related products, formerly dominated by both IBM and DEC.

Developers of client-server networking environments, although unclear in the 80's which networking model to follow, eventually adopted the OSI model in defining and designing their networks in the 90's.

The result is that the smaller and cheaper hardware and software now made by any computer network manufacturer had the high-potential prospect of being fully compatible with any standards-compliant manufacturer's corresponding products. Companies like IBM and DEC had to reorganize, retool and reprice their products to be OSI compliant in order to stay in the business. This boded well for us consumers as competition and standardization brought down computer network product prices. Lower prices then fueled more buying which made for an even greater deployment of computer network technology across all of society.

The OSI computer network model has had a major impact on the evolution of the computer network. It's a great example of the SCFB Paradox. And it is a model that provides direction into an area which in many ways is still abstract and unclear. Understanding the actua specifications and rules of the OSI model can be a challenge, even to the well-informed.

Protocols & Procedures

The majority of my students over the years find the OSI model to be largely theoretical and unclear. In fact, I did not truly comprehend the OSI model until my second year of graduate school. But our purpose here is to know that the OSI model exists. And it specifies the requirements for computer networking along standards-based lines. This results in specific protocols and procedures for doing networks. That is, in specifying hardware and software requirements to do networking in standardized ways.

For example, to connect to the Internet, any OSI compliant hardware that can support connection to the Internet transport, such as a modem or a dedicated connection off of a corporate network, would be OSI compliant.

But the software it requires supporting connectivity to the Internet transport be called TCP/IP. TCP/IP is known as 'protocol' software. The meaning for this most brutal of acronym's is Transmission Control Protocol / Internet Protocol. TCP/IP is actually a group or, as they say, a 'suite of protocols'. But the two main protocols in the package are TCP and IP, that is the logic behind why they named it TCP/IP.

Depending on how the user chooses to connect to the Internet and what the user chooses to do, TCP/IP calls in different protocols which are loaded into memory to support the desired connectivity. The protocols being loaded and used in any given instance, are, for the most part, 'transparent' to the user.

Perhaps the single most important factor in the popularity and growth of the Internet is that it doesn't care how you physically get connected, as long as it is OSI compliant. And it requires TCP/IP protocol software which is made to run on any manufacturer's hardware, regardless of which manufacturer makes the particular brand of TCP/IP you may be running. (Today there are numerous and significant makers of the TCP/IP suite of protocols. Some you have to purchase, others are freeware.)

Part of the problem with the other 'proprietary' network models which have been developed, and perhaps the major reason why they are failing to catch on, (and over the next few years will die out,) is that these other models require you the customer to purchase their particular brand of both the hardware and protocol software. Proprietary models are not 'open'.

Although the OSI model is perhaps the single most important computer network standards development, in the past 40 years, a proliferation of standards have been promulgated covering all the requirements specified in the OSI standard.

Every network technology on the market these days is based on being compliant with or compatible with one or more prevalent industry standards. There are standards to cover all modem types as well as all the other network interfaces, and to cover many and numerous other network components and processes.

Networks are inherently based on "protocols". That is, for the modem connection process and any other type of Network connection process today, there are corresponding protocol requirements. The Internet, for example, requires the use of TCP/IP.

A protocol, by default, specifies the rules and procedures for networking. Protocols are defined through the hardware and software needed to support connectivity. A protocol supports a particular method and type of network connection. It is helpful to view protocol from the following two perspectives.

One, is to view a protocol from the manufacturer's perspective. The manufacturer produces the hardware and/or software to be compliant with one or more protocols. This means that circuits, signal voltage, transistors, flash ROM etc., must all function in particular ways when it is run according to the specified protocol procedures. This is the 'engineering end' of the protocol development process.

Relative to the embedded chip component of the Y2K set of problems, these chips must be capable of processing a 4-BYTE calendar year, or be adjusted through the software or other means to correctly process a 2-BYTE calendar year as if it were 4 BYTEs. The same applies to the general hardware component of the Y2K problem set.

We can say then, that the rule or protocol, for processing calendar year data has changed. We have a new standard in light of Y2K. But there are numerous changes in protocols all the time. The Y2K calendar year field rule is but one in a sea of many and numerous changes that are a routine part of network
Hardware manufacturing life.

The second perspective is the end-user perspective. If the user installs and operates the technology as specified by the procedures provided by the manufacturer, then it should function as designed. That is to say, it should work, and you should be able to connect over the desired network, running the required protocols. Id it is abstract and vague to you, I can understand why.

Every form of networking these days has an accompanying set of protocols that it will support.

The names of the various protocols become very technical very fast. Therefore I'm not going to bore you with much detail on protocols. For example, in order to connect to a particular network, like the World Wide Web, your computer, at the very least, will need to have installed and must be running the TCP/IP protocols, also known as the Internet protocols. Or, as we say for short these days, 'IP'. Your computer can run other protocols, but at a minimum it will need TCP/IP to use the WEB. So you would need to have installed on your computer the TCP/IP software.

The good news is that network service providers these days build in and/or provide to you the protocol software that you need. And they make it easy for you to install. You can guess why they are so 'generous'. Essentially these providers want you to connect into their networks and use their services. Remember, time is money. Generally speaking, the longer you stay connected, the more bandwidth you use, the more money the network provider makes-off of you!

Running the IP protocol on your computer means that you have to use certain procedures, that at times vary, based on what features or functions you are trying to accomplish. It is useful to understand that there are different types of protocols. And process and procedures change, based on protocol type.

It may help to understand protocols by viewing the protocols associated with a non-technical network. Our example with the U. S. Postal System serves as a great process to illustrate protocols. Specifically, the process of mailing a letter. What are the standards, procedures and process?

You need an envelope. You write your letter and seal it inside the envelope. The sender must write the address on the center of the face of the envelope. The sender writes a return address on the upper left corner on the face of the envelope. The sender must place a stamp on the upper right corner of the face side of the envelope. The sender must submit the prepared envelope to the U.S. Postal system, that is, 'mail the envelope'. The system hopefully processes and transports the envelope accordingly, so that it reaches its destination address.

The IP protocol and all other network protocols are very much analogous to the non-technical protocols I described earlier in mailing a letter using the U. S. Postal System. The IP protocol uses different technical steps to complete the corresponding tasks like addressing, translating, stamping, transmitting, etc. The technical term for this is 'encapsulation'. And with networking protocols, everything is encoded at the BIT level in binary 'HIGH' and 'LOW' pulses. And the protocol software takes care of all the encapsulation details for you.

Process and procedure accompany protocol(s) too. As such, networks are intrinsically "Protocolular". My spell checker has marked the term as incorrectly spelled, but this will correct itself in time as more users get used to the term, and like other expediently created computer and network-related terms, it becomes a part of our technoculture. I'm adding the suffix "ular" to the word protocol. But the point is, that networks, in all of their many forms, have one or more protocol requirements that need to be complied with by the manufacturer's hardware and software, as well as the end-user when accessing the network and using the network's resources.

Protocols specify the resulting type of vehicle required. Or, if you will, from the letter-mailing analogy, the ensuing construction, or as we say, the encapsulation of the 'envelope' that gets electronically sent out over the network. And the same protocols specify how the envelope gets decomposed or de-encapsulated once it reaches its network destination.

The protocols required for connecting over a particular network determine what hardware and software you need at your end. That is, where your computer is located, in order to operate over the protocol- specified network. And there are protocols to cover innumerable methods of network connectivity.

If your primary requirement is to connect to and use network-X for example, determine what protocol(s) you need for network-X. Then base your hardware and software purchase decisions on acquiring those systems that include these particular protocols. This includes networking information or data, video, as in video-conferencing, and voice, as in various telephone types. All of these options have particular protocol requirements for end-users to meet in order to network. Each have hardware and software components. And although our focus here is computer networks, it is useful to recognize that the same transport can and will be used for data, voice and video,-each media having its own set of respective protocols. And whether it is data, voice or video; its all BITs, once it is placed on the network for transmission.

You might guess that the term protocol was derived from the more formal definition that is applied frequently in the State Department, particularly in governing the interaction between or among different countries through their respective ambassadors. It is essentially the same term, except that with networks, it takes on a whole new technical perspective.

Elements including hardware, software, connection method, transmission rate, how BITs & BYTEs are packaged for transmission over the network, etc., are governed by a variety of protocol specifications. And these make their way out to the marketplace in the form of hardware and software products, and in the services delivered to companies and consumers by network providers.

The good news is that once a protocol is made to comply with the official standard(s) governing its method of connection,end-users like ourselves can readily determine what is required on our end to initiate and complete the given network connection. Organizations can also evaluate, define or modify their corporate network infrastructures based on standards and their accompanying protocols. Believe it or not, this helps bring down the overall costs of networking. And it increases consumption, because users now know in certain terms what they need to network in ways that will meet their requirements.

On the corporate side, 'scalability', or how the network can be modified to fit changing needs cost-effectively over time, becomes a much more palatable option with chosen networks that are supported by well defined standards and protocols. If a technology is said to be OSI compliant, this is an indication that it is going to run with most, if not all other types of network hardware and software.

16

Network Summary

As you can see from the summary in the previous chapter, we have come a long way in developing smaller, cheaper, faster and better (SCFB) network technologies. From the slowest and cheapest of modems making use of the public switched voice transport infrastructure to the high end SONET and OC-12 based transports, we have far surpassed the limitations of networking that prevailed during the early days. As we read, there are now OC-48, and OC-192 transports which take us even further in bandwidth and throughput capabilities.

And we can now integrate data networking as well as video and voice on the same transport. This makes for high innovation in terms of optimizing the networking overhead cost savings for both consumers and corporations. If we can send and receive multi-media (i.e. data, video, voice) signals over the same singular transport, we can bring about tremendous savings, because in effect, we would eliminate the overhead associated with each of these 3 separate media transports and replace it with only one transport cost. However, many criteria, including usage patterns and network traffic volumes current and anticipated, need to be considered in designing an integrated solution. Still, this is the direction of networking technology.

Although the type of protocols and transports available for support of the network vary by bandwidth capability, cost expressed in dollars, and the types of applications which can be operated, there are 5 essential elements of networking that can be applied to any networking transport option. These 5 elements generally help to bring out the essential presuppositions associated with networking across the board. BITs & BYTEs can be visualized in all 5 elements. The 5 elements are:

1) BIT Overhead

2) Network Transport

3) Standards

4) Protocol(s)

5) Process & Procedure

Up to this point, I have used the modem to bring out and illustrate many concepts related to BITs & BYTEs, particularly as related to the computer' s main Data BUS and networking. Now I would like to continue my use of the modem to illustrate the above 5 essential elements of networking. Once again, the modem enables us to discuss these essentials from a modem perspective while conveying the analogous meanings for networking up through the massively powerful and superfast MegaBIT and GigaBIT networks.

BIT Overhead

Earlier, I covered how the modem type of transport has BIT overhead allied with transporting each and every meaningful BYTE across the public switched voice network transport. This overhead adds cost to networking because more BITs are required. This means that it will take more time to transport, and time is money, particularly on a dialup, public switched network transport.

Even if it is not a long-distance modem call; (say a flat rate for metropolitan service), and the remote computer host you are dialing into is physically located in the same or general area as the location you are dialing from, the host computer you may be dialing into may charge you for the total time you are connected. This is how the Internet Service Providers (ISP) charge.

With an ISP, you can pay a much higher flat monthly fee and then are permitted to have unlimited time on their network. Or you can pay a fee based on actual connect time.

The point here is that modem-based dial-up via the public

switched transport, (which is the same transport used to support telephone calls, only with telephones) is available, and works, but has costs associated with it. The bps, or bandwidth capabilities, need to be assessed relative to what you are planning to accomplish using any method of network transport.

This assessment, if it is done properly, comes down to calculating BITs and BYTEs. In this way you will know, based on good estimates, what kind of BIT & BYTE capacity you require. If you know this, then you can select and optimize the appropriate network transport to support your networking needs cost-effectively.

What if you are going to be dialing into a host computer located on the West Coast from your home located on the East Coast? This would be a major toll call. And depending on the time you were going to be connected, it could cost a small fortune. So, if it is your only alternative, then you would want to estimate total cost. You do this by estimating total BITs to be transmitted. Total BITs is a function of total BYTEs + total overhead BITs.

Let's say you were going to do file transfers every day at a certain time using dialup access. How many BYTEs are in each of the files to be transferred? Calculate total BITs from meaningful BYTEs? You need to know what kind of BYTEs (i.e. EBCDIC, ASCII, mathematical, etc.) Then add the overhead BITs: 1 START, 1 STOP, and 1 or none depending on whether or not you are running parity—per BYTE to be transmitted.

If you know total BITs to be transported, and you know the speed of your modem as expressed in BITs-per-second, you can calculate how long it is going to take you to complete the file transfer(s).

What is the cost of connecting via dial-up at the specific times you want to complete the file transfer(s)? Remember long distance carriers change rates based on time of day. Can you do the transfers at a time when the rates are the lowest? This requires some coordination with the folks on the other end. But it could be worth it in terms of total dollar costs. If you know the rates your long-distance carrier will be charging you by the time of day, you can calculate what your total cost will be to complete these file transfers.

Does the destination end have modem access on a toll free 800 or 888 number? Voila! Toll free. You can connect at no cost. (Many ISPs, that is Internet Service Providers, provide toll free dial up access). It is an incentive for you to connect up. It is intuitive. Why? Because they charge by total connect time. As such, overhead BITs become very important, because you ideally want to move only meaningful information BYTEs most economically.

And these ISPs have all kinds of ads and offers coming onto your screen at login, at logoff, and some while you are connected. The latest CD-ROM on sale at whatever....click here if interested....or click there if not interested. I see some government regulation eventually controlling this situation. How much of this total BIT load relates to meaningful information BYTEs for you the customer?

Clearly, then, BIT overhead adds overhead cost to your networking applications. The good news is that with dial-up networking you can plan for the most cost-effective options for doing the above file transfers and any other applications which are compatible with dial-up. Know your options.

And you can use the same methods above for determining your total costs with any dial-up application. Keep in mind 2 things about the dial-up method over the public switched transport. First, it is the slowest of transport options, but it is the most flexible. Second, depending on how you use it, it could very well be the cheapest. In general terms, it is the cheapest. But I've seen some pretty hefty phone bills that related back to poor use of modems and the switched dialup network transport.

Network Transport

The dial-up method, though slow and cheap, can be very effective in support of your networking transport needs. However there are many applications that will not work over the public switched transport.

And to fulfill the burgeoning need by consumers and companies to run diverse multi-media applications running high-bandwidth applications many other network transport technologies have evolved. These are summarized in Chapter 14. Formulas of simple construction using total BITs, total BYTEs and total overhead BYTEs can be developed and applied to each and every transport technology.

The point is that the transport is an important essential element of networks. Yes, it is analogous to the highway. The main Data BUS of the computer is analogous to the network transport in the sense that is constitutes the main highway over which all of the overhead BITs and meaningful BYTEs get transferred to their respective network destination.

There are varying costs associated with the network transport. Costs in dollars for setting up the transport service. Cost in terms of quality of service, (based on infrastructure uptime, throughput (i.e. response time), ease of use, and costs for regular recurring use of the transport. Dedicated transports typically cost more to set up. In addition, there is a recurring monthly charge. Also, there may or may not be costs for total time of connection or total BITs transferred. Do overhead BITs get included if you are charged by the BIT? Of course!

All of these factors and questions need to be considered in selecting a network transport. And the network transport is a requirement for any type networking. There is a major distinction between switched and dedicated transport services. Nevertheless, any network requires at least one, or both used in combination, to support overall networking transport requirements.

Standards

The net effect of standards on networking has been good. Standards minimize compatibility issues, and therefore, by extension, customer woes. You buy products and services based on a standard, versus what any particular vendor thinks you need to buy. The result is that we eliminate potential for buying the wrong thing. With every manufacturer making hardware and software to meet standard specifications, it means increased production capabilities, lowering costs for production and increasing competition for making the same product and/or selling the same service. All of which bodes well for the economy as well as the consumer and corporate network buyer. This essentially means lower prices and better services. Once again, smaller, cheaper, faster and presumably better, the SCFB paradox.

Standards result in the development and deployment of protocols. Networks, as I explained earlier are inherently 'protocolular'. A protocol specifies the rules and procedures for operational use. Protocols are programmed into the software and hardware at the machine level. Protocols make their way upward to us human technology users largely in the form of procedures.

To implement, for example, the IEEE 802 set of network standards, the network would need to be designed to run the minimal protocols required for the IEEE 802 network environment. (IEEE is short for Institute for Electrical and Electronic Engineers. The IEEE is a highly regarded standards certifying organization.) This means that all hardware and software needs to be compatible with the IEEE 802 standard protocols. If the hardware and software meet the IEEE 802 specifications then we say that these products are IEEE 802 compliant. If it turns out that they are not compliant, the buyer has the right to a full refund.

Protocols

Protocols are the rules for specifying everything from how the technology will process the signal voltage at the machine level on up to how the end user will install software to connect to the network. Embedded in the protocol are the minimal hardware and software requirements. Knowing what protocols a company is running on behalf of its network, says a lot to the network engineer about the soul and substance of that company's network. Knowing the protocols being run to the engineer means knowing the true limitations of the network and how to overcome these limitations.

The protocol rules can take the form of hardware and/or software. It is commonplace for networking gurus to think of protocols mainly as software. That is what we refer to as "drivers". Drivers are software executable programs that run on the computer to encapsulate or packetize the signal voltage going out onto the network in a specific way. I mentioned TCP/IP earlier. This is what TCP/IP's major function is. Some of the other competitive protocols to TCP/IP would be IPX and IBM's SNA. All three are software.

But all three of these imply great differences in the type of block, packet or envelope, if you will, that go out onto the network. There are differences in the overhead BITs required. There are differences in the non-overhead total BYTEs carried per container (i.e. packet, block, envelope, frame). And potential differences in the hardware and software that the network is supporting. IBM SNA protocols, for example, imply directly that there is an IBM mainframe somewhere on the network.

Also, since protocol is another word for rules that take the form of software and hardware, it has become appropriate in the network domain of people to refer to software and hardware in generic protocol categories. With modem dial-up type connections, reference can correctly be made to this type of protocol set as being "supportive of dial-up protocols'. So if you're techy enough, you know right away that you are talking about a technology that is at slow speed, low cost and flexible, as previously discussed.

Or you hear statements like, 'the company is running ATM protocols'. Right away you know enough to know that the company has a huge investment in place for super-high bandwidth, multimedia ATM networking. ATM, or Asynchronous Transfer Mode technology, especially over the wide area network, is very expensive right now, (i.e. well over 6 figures for startup costs alone for just a few sites) and requires more bandwidth to support than most of the other prevailing transport technologies today. On the flip side, any protocol can be made to run over an ATM network transport, including those that govern video and voice. This is the kind of transport it would take today to run, for example, a state-wide network of hospitals supporting thousands of users, including surgeons that can video-conference from their desktop computers with any of the other surgeons on the network. Also, this is the kind of network that uses the same transport for not only video-conferencing, but voice, that is, telephone and data networking, as well.

Therefore as a result, protocols are an essential element of networks. One which needs to be evaluated in any network evolution from the most simple of changes to larger and more costly modifications to the enterprise's overall design. Cost, functionality and existing investments in hardware and software all need to be considered relative to any decisions on protocols.

Protocols dictate what the procedure will be for loading the respective 'driver' programs so that the computer will be readied for doing its network thing(s) according to standard specification.

And protocols guide how the user will proceed in connecting up to the network. Protocols are like the engine on a long string of railroad cars. Protocols determine to a large extent how all the other railroad cars must comply with the protocol engine in order to be transported over the rail system.

Process & Procedure

Time of day to connect to the network has become an ever increasing network operation criterion. It might be that the applications involved are more cost-effectively processed at night when there is limited production use of the network. Or it may be that the application over the network needs to run during production in order to support all of the users that may be on this network from around the country in doing their jobs.

Networking from the user perspective is all 'process'. Using the modem example one last time, you can see that there is a process with starting up your computer, connecting to the network, running applications on the network, logging off the network and lastly, shutting down your computer.

Process(es) are defined as a result of standards which mandate specific protocols, that have clear procedures associated with them. It is helpful to view networking as a set of processes. It seems far removed from the explanation I gave on how BITs are generated, or how BYTEs get transferrred over the network, but it is process nevertheless.

The tendency in our society these days is to view networking, even networking via a modem, as 'point and click'. The fact is, that by viewing your networking method as a process, you will force yourself to visualize and consider the procedures you use, and the protocols you will load in order to connect to specific network applications. It also compels you to treat the network and its resources as separate entities from your own computer. By doing this you can more readily comprehend where problems may lie if and when problems develop, and you will be likely to monitor the networking costs you incur even as you are connected.

Y2K related requirements will bring about some necessary changes in the way we do networking. No doubt about it. And, it will be across the board impacting all networks. But, you know what, many changes have come before Y2K. And, many changes will impact networking life beyond the year 2000.

Change is a way of life in networks and telecommunications. Those of us who work in the field know this precept quite well. Long hours, including weekends, to bring the network down, to install a new change, test it out, and bring the network back up for production use the next working day. This is how networks are maintained. Y2K will certainly be a challenge to the ordinary stuff, but it is not anything that will scare those of us who work with change on a daily basis.

Lastly, I think it is useful to consider Y2K in terms of the 5 constructs of network life I have discussed herein.

Will Y2K have an impact on the BIT overhead of Networks? The answer is yes. Obviously if we now transmit 4-BYTEs, instead of 2-BYTEs to process the calendar year that adds the corresponding amount of BITs to any such network transmission. No big deal though! We have networks transmitting multiple billions of BITs on a daily continual basis all over the country. I would not be converting my bank savings to gold coins over this one.

Also, depending on how a particular company remediates its network systems, they may still continue to use the 2-BYTE version of the year, and correct the problem at either end of network transmission through the software programming. I detail the software fixes to Y2K in Part IV of this book. So in this case no additional BIT overhead is added to the network.

Some say that networks will be failing all over because of Y2K. This is possible and certainloy probable. In companies where remediation did not occur, incorrect results, stoppages and other potentialities can take place come Y2K. This can drive up the overhead cost of running a network. But, this is not a direct function of the number of required BITs & BYTEs to support Y2K. This is a result of poor management. And, networks like anything else require maintenance. Networks fail. Networks get fixed. Life goes on.

Will Y2K have an impact on Network Transports? Absolutely! Organizations will need to remediate, where appropriate, there network transport infrastructures. This has been going on for many years. Some companies we know, have not done anything at all to remediate for Y2K. Many countries in the world, we know, have not done anything! This is somewhat scary. But we are going to get through it. Companies that have not taken care of their Y2K network transport requirements are going to have problems. It is as simple as that.

I have completed many projects, as of this date, in helping organizations upgrade and modify their network transports to be Y2K compliant. I know many other consultants out there doing the same. It requires assessment and inventory of the organization's hardware and software, identifying what needs to take place (i.e. usually component(s) replacement, upgrade or what you got is Y2K OK), and developing an action-project plan to get it all done. In many cases where replacement is needed, it is needed irrespective of Y2K anyway.

I also know that many organizations, in particular, small businesses and local governments, are not doing much of anything in terms of Y2K.

This is somewhat understandable, because in these segments there are limited resources to get the job done, and typically they do not have the kind of revenue that permits them to bring in an outsource-consultant. I am not sure what the answer is for these organizations. We can expect some problems form this segment of our economy come Y2K.

How does Y2K relate to networking standards? Y2K standards have already been defined and promulgated for over two years. Some may say we knew about Y2K for over three decades. How come it is only recently that we have Y2K related standards? Where was the government on this? Why did the OSI model not incorporate Y2K? Good points. Simply said, we missed it on this one. Everyone, the government as well as the information technology industry should have had better vision.

But, today we have a standard specifying Y2K requirements. To summarize it for you here, the standard says that systems, network or stand-alone, will not malfunction due to the calendar year changing from a 2-digit year to a 4-digit year. It specifies that operations will continue to operate as normal, before, during and after the millennium date change. Lastly, it requires that in order to be considered compliant, systems must store, process and retrieve, year related information consistently across all operations. A point worth bringing out further is, the standard provides for the acceptance of a 2-digit year, as long as this data does not disrupt operations. We will see a lot of 2-digit years with the processing of credit cards. However, it will come down to whether or not the responsible bank has remediated their network/systems to process the 2-digit year (i.e. 00, 01, etc.) correctly. The same can be said for a 4-digit year on a credit card. Both year types can bring out problems if remediation has not occurred. The Y2K standard is clear. Actually, it is much more lucid than many standards that we have been required to implement in networks.

Moreover, with network protocols, the Y2K standard is straightforward. The protocols in use on a network will operate to encapsulate network transmissions, regardless of what is in the year field. Like in our example earlier with the U. S. mail and the envelope. The protocols in use do not care what I put in the envelope, so to speak, they will do their thing anyway. So, it is mainly at the source and terminating end points of a network connection that the Y2K standards-compliant information needs to be processed.

Finally, with network process and procedures, we can expect to see numerous changes. This is because we have become a society very much dependent on information technology. Just about everything is in one way or another connected over a network. When we buy groceries, charge a piece of furniture, buy gas, pay our mortgage, get our paycheck, etc.

It is a Y2K-probability that many organizations will not have taken care of their Y2K remediation business. Consequently, we can expect that those of us on the Y2K-compliant-side, as well as the general public, will need to make adjustments in our network-related processes and procedures. How and what exactly the procedural adjustments will be, cannot be determined until we actually get to Y2K. And I expect such changes to continue subsequently beyond Y2K for several years thereafter. We will not resolve all Y2K problems by January 1, 2000. But we will eventually resolve them.

Given that we have covered the BIT, BYTE and the Network, we are now ready to deal with the Y2K set of problems.

PART IV: Year 2000 (Y2K)

17

Y2K Problem Summary

As of this writing there are just 435 days left until the Year 2000. There seems to be more concern with who will pay for the 40 Million-dollar Starr investigation than there is with the 40 Billion embedded system microchips, of which 2%-10% will be non-compliant, come Y2K. The prospective list of problems that could be caused by non-compliant embedded system microchips is endless. The potential is there to affect any computer, any software program, running over any network, in every city, county, state, and country. And, it is not just computers per se. It is everything controlled by electronic components. Because, if electronic, then they have embedded system microchips: same for transportation systems. Gas pipeline systems which ultimately provide heat to your home could fail. Small devices, large devices. Scanners, readers, ATM machines, telephone systems-even your TV, VCR and the very timepiece you may be wearing on your wrist-could shut down. These things could be unavailable for your use for 1, 2 or even 3 days at a time. This would cause a lot of frustration, time loss, confusion, and I am sure ultimately, it would add to the cost of many commodities and services.

But I would advise that you not go into survival mode. It will not be that bad. Following is my definition of the Y2K set of problems. I know much work is being done, and today many organizations are already Y2K compliant. Still, much work is needed in many sectors of the economy. I developed my definition from the perspective of Y2K problem priorities. This is the set of priorities I use when I assess a company's Y2K status.

Y2K IS MUCH MORE THAN A COMPUTER PROBLEM

Because much of society is dependent on electronic components, many systems and components are at risk. Most people who have heard of Y2K have developed the perception that it is purely a computer problem. Some call it the "Millenium Bug". This is not accurate.

We have misdiagnosed the extent of the Y2K problem! We failed to PRIORITIZE the set of Y2K problems! We did not and are not solving the problems in the correct order. We have applied a computer problem paradigm to a socio-technological impasse! As such, we have never before in our society had a problem of such enormous magnitude, in which at the same time we had so many varying perceptions about what the problem is and what is needed to be done to resolve it. Consequently, our Y2K priorities are all mixed up!

We were lulled to sleep on the Y2K problem because, as the thinking goes, anything that can operate at nearly the speed of light, surely can correct itself automatically.

We truly reveal as a society how little we know about the computer, including its manifest and its latent dysfunction's. The computer was not originally supposed to infiltrate every aspect of socio-economic life. The computer was designed initially to make mathematical calculations. Consequently, the broader-based implications of Y2K have been sorely underestimated. And if we do not act swiftly over the next 15 months, we as a society will be faced with unpredictable consequences.

In business everything from accounts payable to warehouse order control is computerized. In health-care everything from medical administration to radiology is automated and on-line. And almost everything computerized in organizations today is also on some kind of a computer network which enables more real-time, direct sharing and transfer of information between organizations in electronic form. Consequently, today on the near eve of Y2K, there are very few organizations that can operate without computerization. This includes banks, hospitals, utility companies, government, manufacturing, transportation, the military, grocery store chains, and so on. Most organizations of religious worship, (i.e. churches, temples, etc.) today you will find have computers supporting their administration.

As the technology got smaller, cheaper, faster, better, and on a network, we discovered that computer technology could be used to automate and control many functions that heretofore required the manual intervention of a human being.

Should we be worried? If it is smaller, cheaper, faster and better than ever before, should that not be a good thing? Quite simply, if it is not Y2K compliant, it is defective. Not only that, if it is not Y2K compliant, it can cause compliant computer systems with which it must interoperate to become defective. Y2K ready organizations are well-advised to put in place adequate security systems, especially on their networks that connect out to the rest of the world, such as with Internet and other companies, like in their supply chains. I believe network security should be a part of the overall Y2K remediation strategy.

We know that computers today are smaller, cheaper, faster and better. We also know that the chips that run them are faster and more powerful then ever before. Some people think that computerization can be concealed anywhere, anyone can buy it, it is never slow, and it is always a 'good thing'. Well, we are about to find out! Certainly some perspective is needed here to truly understand the scope of the problem and the appropriate priorities we must take in order to solve the Y2K problem.

Y2K IS AN EMBEDDED SYSTEM CHIP PROBLEM

Y2K from its inception is essentially a digit-storage problem! We have been using, designing, deploying, and developing computer systems for over 50 years that code the calendar year field using-the last 2 digits of the year. For example, 1998 would be coded as 98. This works fine as it is for now. The problem(s), to occur, will be when we reach the Year 2000. Any non-compliant computer systems which cannot process the year as a 4-digit field will shut down or yield incorrect results in completing any calculations which use the computer's stored date field.

It really comes down to the "storage" of a 2-digit calendar year field versus a 4-digit calendar year field. With the inception of the vacuum tube-based computers back in the early days, circa 1940s, the technology was not equipped to store large amounts of digits the way the technology is today. Storage in itself has been in evolution since the 1940s. Just 25 years ago it cost $10,000 to store 1-million BYTEs of information (1-digit equals 1-BYTE). Today it costs less than ten cents to store the same amount of BYTEs.

Consequently early computer scientists got into the haBIT of taking translation shortcuts to "code" information into the "storage-limited" computer. One of these shortcuts was to code the calendar year using the last 2-digits instead of all four. As the storage technology improved, the coding of the calendar year using the last 2-digits...stuck. The rationale was that using a 2-digit calendar year saved 2-digits of storage and 2-BYTEs of main memory. This meant easier and cheaper to store and faster to process. As a result, all of the subsequent computer and computer network hardware was manufactured to support the 2-digit calendar year field.

You may wonder how electronic devices can remember the date and time. You turn it off. Then turn it back on. It comes back up with the correct date and time. How does it remember the date and time? The manufacturer installs certain microchips that track time and dates within the computer and numerous other electronic devices. These chips continue to keep on ticking even when the power is turned off. They have become known as 'embedded systems'. Onboard rechargeable batteries power them when the main power is turned off. Once your computer or network hardware is set up with the current date and time, it keeps track from then on with amazing accuracy. And until Y2K became an issue, all of these embedded system chips were manufactured to store the calendar year as a 2-digit field.

Industry estimates indicate that there have been over 40 billion embedded system microchips sold of the kind that keep and track time and date stamps. It is further estimated that between 2% - 10% of these microchips **are not** Y2K compliant. Now on the surface this may not seem like a big problem. After all, this means that over 36 billion embedded systems are indeed Y2K compliant.

So why worry? Well, until 1995, we did not track where these embedded systems were installed. It takes one microchip on one network to cause a major outage. One non-compliant embedded chip can terminate natural gas supplies to a significant geographical region. These pipeline systems use electronic switches controlled by date sensitive embedded system chips. And there are numerous other prospective examples. Remember, we have at least 800 million, and as many as 4 billion embedded chips that are not compliant. That's a lot of chips!

A current fear that continues to show up in the media regarding Y2K is that the average passenger jet has over 160 embedded system chips, and that there may be problems with 'planes falling from the sky'. This is completely ridiculous!

The pilot and crew ultimately control these aircraft. They do meticulous pre and post flight checks on every flight. They are required to do so

Furthermore, it is true that planes have many embedded chips, but none of them can take control of the aircraft away from the pilot. And, you should know that today, all electronic components have embedded chips. Some systems do have embedded chips that do control system operation. Like, for example, on switches that controls the flow of natural gas and water. These system chips control because they are set to shutdown by default when they cannot calculate the correct date stamp. And we will experience some outagess as a result. Again, these outages could last for 1-3 days. The good news is that these chips can replaced within fifteen minutes.

Similarly, these embedded system microchips are used to control other functions. Bank vault doors and numerous other types of doors, subway tickets, ATM banking machines, and credit card processors use them. Ever notice the transaction date on your monthly credit card bill?

There are embedded chips in trains and automobiles. In healthcare, where analysts maintain most systems are lagging behind or have not yet begun any Y2K redemption, there are numerous embedded system microchips. They are used in such areas as clinical laboratory services, radiology systems and pharmacy services to support time and date stamping. All organizations have HVAC (i.e. heating, ventilation, cooling) systems which use them. The list goes on ad infinitum.

Y2K IS A HARDWARE PROBLEM

Although perhaps the most critical, the problem is not just the embedded systems. Much of the older computer and network- related hardware is non-compliant, cannot be made to be compliant and will need to be replaced by the Year 2000. This, believe it or not, is the simplest of the Y2K set of problems.

It is simple because we know what we need to do with hardware. Take inventory, balance the inventory against the manufacturer's Y2K compliance list using model, and or serial numbers to determine remediation requirements.

After completing this, it then comes down to that each hardware component asset you have either needs replacement, or upgrade or what you got is Y2K compliant. This is pretty straightforward.

In the last 6 months approximately, many software packages have hit the market that actually do this for you. If you buy one of these software packages, install it on your network, it will go out and read from the network in, every single component attached to your network. The system then gives you a list, mainly by node-address number, of each component. The list tells you in plain English, what components are Y2K-ready, which are not, and which can be upgraded to be ready.

Given this, you would think that most organizations would be near or at total Y2K readiness. But that is not the case. It is true that the hardware side of Y2K is easier to correct, but there can be complications in larger organizations where there is a large degree of operational dependence on mainframe systems.

In response to criticism about not taking any action to remediate its non-compliant mainframe computer systems, the FAA issued a statement that it is not remediating their mainframes because it already has plans to replace them with Y2K compliant-ready systems. Now these are not PCs that fit on the desktop. These are systems that take up a good part of a room. Many of these mainframes are interconnected across the country. They are used to support the air traffic control network in this country. Airport and radar grids depend on the FAA network. Experienced professionals in the computer industry will tell you that to migrate in and convert onto a new mainframe requires an 18-36 month systems life cycle. We have 435 days left until Y2K! That's exactly 15 months. That represents a REAL problem! Will they be able to fix it? Stay tuned.

Y2K IS A SOFTWARE PROBLEM

On the software side, it is a matter of taking inventory (auditing) to determine what programs require remediation or replacement. Remediation in the software sense means to change the computer program instruction codes to accommodate or calculate the calendar year using 4 digits. There is a distinction to be made in the types of software.

At the consumer level, most software is what we call 'application oriented'. That means, it is software that has been preprogrammed at the factory in one or more programming languages, and packaged for selling to you the consumer. There are lots of examples from e-mail packages up through word-processing, spreadsheeting and numerous others. Typically, consumers buy application software to be compatible with the computer hardware that they expect to run it on. As such, if your hardware is Y2K compliant, and if you buy compatible software, you should be fine. Older software packages will not necessarily be Y2K compliant. These software packages will not, most likely, run on your, Y2K compliant hardware. Therefore, there is not expected to be much of a problem, if at all, with application software at the consumer level. On older hardware, check with your dealer or manufacturer regarding compliance.

Conversely, for the past 5 decades, software application programs that have been developed for commerce continued to use the calendar year shortcut. This type of software runs on the more expensive types of hardware. Million dollar mainframes, connected to multi-million dollar networks are a good example. I'm not just referring to one company or one government agency. It is all organizations. Not all organizations have million dollar networks, but a large percentage of them do. Even the smaller organizations with less expensive hardware, for the most part, are running software application programs, which have within them, the coding to process the calendar year as a 2-digit field.

The commerce level includes all of business, government, healthcare and so forth. Over the past 5 decades that the computer has been in evolution, many thousands of unique computer programs have been developed. These programs run the myriad's of applications that support countless organizations needs to automate. Myriad's of functions: from accounting and finance, keeping track of your social security payments, calculating your mortgage finance charges, and determining your principal balance on any given day of the month, as you perhaps well know, have been automated through computer application software. And the vast majority of these software programs were created with the 2-digit calendar year field.

There are so many application software programs out there in commerce that I have not enough space or time to summarize them. But, you can see that even if all of the computer and computer network hardware is brought into Y2K compliance, if the software application programs are processing the calendar year using only the last 2-digits, we have only extended our capability to process and store what will be-incorrect results.

At present there are three techniques used to correct the software. They are "WINDOWING", "ENCAPSULATION" and "EXPANSION".

WINDOWING

Windowing uses software logic to take in a 2-digit year like 00, and then based on pre-programmed routines, it converts it to a 4-digit year, in this case 2000, or another appropriate value depending on what the application is. This technique is not a total solution, requires programming expertise, and will not work with all embedded systems requiring a source year of 4-digits such as like some embedded systems used to control switching devices supporting gas pipelines and other utilities. Also, windowing does not account for all 4-digit years. If the source input on a system is an old year, say the year 1900, in a windowing solution, the system would not know if it should make this the year 1900 or the year 2000. Windowing is the easiest software solution to implement. However, it is the most difficult to manage over time. Windowing should be used with caution, but it's part of the solution. In particular, it will be used extensively with many of the credit card applications. Wondering how a '00' or a '01' expiration year on a credit card is going to work after Y2K? Windowing would be the solution.

ENCAPSULATION

Encapsulation is a technique in which a table of codes is programmed into the system. For example the year 1999 is 99, 2000 is 0A, 2001 is 0B and so forth. Moreover, additional programming is needed to code and decode the input and output of the year fields. Furthermore, encapsulation complicates the way in which an organization would process any archived data (i.e. data already processed and stored under the traditional 2-digit year field). For example, what if you restore some archived data to the system and there are some older dates that do not have a corresponding code? It would be difficult to implement. For a limited number of application systems, particularly if the system has a short life span, encapsulation may be a reasonable solution. Full and complete replacement should then follow with Y2K compliant systems.

EXPANSION

Expansion is by far the most comprehensive solution to the software set of Y2K problems. It is also the most expensive. Essentially, programmers go into every program related to year-date fields, and insert program logic which 'expands' the number of digits used for input and output of year fields from 2 to 4 for every line of code (i.e. LOC) in each and every program that processes year-date fields. Some programs have multiple LOCs or they may have just a single LOC that needs to be expanded.

When I worked for a major retailer with over 500 stores on the eastern seaboard, we had over 35,000 programs. About 31,000 programs were date-related. The average program contained 1,200 LOCs, of which, approximately 6 LOC pertained to this date change. Also remember that making the change, each program then would have to be tested to make sure it ran correctly along with all of the other programs that pertained to its particular system.

Similarly, for the invoicing system, we had 900 other separate programs that ran together or at different operational times. I point this out to give you a glimpse of the enormity of this piece of the software-side problem. Imagine what the larger corporations have to go through. Expansion is the most expensive and the most difficult solution to implement. But the good news is expansion completely solves the software side of the Y2K problem until the year 10000.

More good news is that in the last several months, many software companies have put out on the market software packages that offer automated solutions to the software remediation. In particular, these packages support windowing and expansion. I have not yet seen any that can do encapsulation. But encapsulation is perhaps least in demand. And encapsulation has limited use anyway.

As a result, the earlier costs, which had been thrown about in the media for many months, are now all considered inaccurate. The software remediation cost estimates have come way down. From what used to be over $3 per LOC to 23 cents per LOC. This is really good news! For organizations lagging behind on the software side of the problem, there may be salvation here.

After all, software remediation is the big time consumer. Now, it is possible to automate the process. This does not mean it will not take time. It means that it can greatly reduce the remediation time. The down side is that these particular software packages are not cheap. For mainframe level packages, the cost estimates I gathered, were all into the 6 figure margin. Only one package I found, ranged from 68K up to 85K depending on all the various modules the customer would select.

OTHER Y2K PROBLEMS

Scheduling and calendaring requirements present yet further complications to Y2K, even for the most Y2K responsive organizations. First, the year 2000 is a leap year. Being a leap year does not help the software remediation side of the Y2K set of problems. Software programs, since the early days of the computer, accounted for the leap year. That is they calculated for the leap year by adding a few lines of programming code which tested for leap year by dividing the last 2 digits of the calendar year by 4. If the result was an even number then the calendar year was a leap year. If the result was not divisible by 4 then it was not a leap year. This is called the “leap year algorithm”.

As you may be aware leap years have one more day, 366, than regular calendar years 365. We adjust the total days in the month of February to have 29 days whenever it is a leap year. (An important consideration when you calculate finance charges on the remaining balance of a loan, by the day).

The Year 2000 happens to be a leap year. But the usual algorithm will not work for this year.

That is because you cannot divide 00 by 4. As result the conventional leap year algorithm will not work for the Year 2000. I mention this here because I think it serves to clarify further that the upgrading, conversion and replacement of software programs which need to consider leap year will be more complicated than if a given program did not have to consider leap year. Fortunately, all of the software packages available for remediation have built in routines to account for the need to fix the leap year problem.

Leap year does not pose any problem to Y2K compliant hardware, including embedded systems microchips that are Y2K ready.

Next, it is important to note that January 1, 2000 is a Saturday. Being a weekend means that the special operating procedures governing weekend operations will be in effect at most companies. Will staff be ready to respond to any irregular outages? Will they be ready to bring systems back up when appropriate?

What will they do if it turns out that one or more pieces of hardware in the company contain an embedded chip that is not Y2K compliant? Will the HVAC systems run all weekend or shut down? Are contingencies in place? These important questions need to be addressed. Being a weekend does not help the Y2K cause for commerce.

Also, many private-sector organizations use a fiscal year beginning April 1 or July 1. So in the private sector we may begin to hear of Y2K-related problems as early as the end of the first calendar quarter of 1999.

Moreover, the federal government's fiscal year begins in October of the previous year. This means that although the calendar year will be 1999, the Year 2000 fiscal year will begin on October 1, 1999. As such, we could see numerous problems with government systems early on. This will be a foretaste of what we can expect come January 1, 2000.

Following is a list of Y2K readiness status for all federal government agencies. The U. S. Office of Management and Budget released this report in October 1998. The federal government's progress in remediating its Y2K set of problems across all agencies is that: out of 7,343 mission critical systems, 50% are now Y2K ready, 40% are currently undergoing remediation, 9% are being replaced and 1% will be retired. The Office of Management and Budget does not break out 'mission critical' from all other systems in the following table. However this information is useful in gaining an overall view of where the federal government is with Y2K. Not unexpectedly, the Social Security Administration is at the top of the Y2K readiness list.

FEDERAL GOVERNMENT Y2K READINESS BY DEPARTMENT

DEPARTMENT/AGENCY	% READINESS
Social Security Administration	93
National Science Foundation	82
Environmental Protection Agency	79
General Services Administration	78
Department of Commerce	76
Small Business Administration	74
Federal Emergency Management	69
Department of Agriculture	63
NASA	63
Department of Veterans Affairs	61
Housing and Urban Development	60
Office of Personnel Management	48
Department of Transportation	46
Department of Treasury	45
Department of Defense	42
Health and Human Services	41
Department of Energy	40
Department of Labor	39
State Department	36
Department of the Interior	32
Justice Department	32
Department of Education	29
Nuclear Regulatory Commission	29
Agency for International Development	14

*Source: U.S. Office of Management and Development

Lastly, I want to say a few words about the Global Positioning System (GPS) issue that has been thrown about in the media. GPS is the network of satellites that we have out there in space running 24 by 7 hours a week. GPS is essential to our worldwide communications, entertainment, defense and other applications. There is some concern that we may have problems with what is called 'Week Number Roll Over' (WNRO). But, I think these concerns are again exaggerated.

It is true that on August 21, 1999, the GPS system will need to reset its week assignment counter. When started the GPS week assignment was based on a counter that ran from 0-1023. If you do the math you will see that 1023 corresponds with the week of August 21, 1999. In other words, the counter will be reaching its end. Fortunately, in this case, the counter can be reset to then continue to reassign the weeks on a sequential basis.

My understanding with this problem, is that it is under control. It cannot be implemented and tested until that time. This is a concern. But contingencies are in place to buy time, so to speak, if they run into problems come August, 1999. If downtime is necessary it will be minimal, that is, less than 12 hours.

Finally, we had a foretaste of satellite failure recently. Remember this past year when all the pagers of the world were not working because of satellite software malfunction. If you do I congratulate you. I have been asking many people to see what kind of an impact it had on their daily lives. Not too many people even heard about it, let alone did it impact their daily life at all. I know I for one was "greatly upset" that my pager was not beeping continually all day. Other than that I really did not notice any disruption. I do recall getting a lot of work done that day.

SUMMARY

In my opinion with the entire Y2K set of problems, we are lacking in leadership and media coverage on the macro level. Monday 10/19/1998, President Clinton signed The Readiness and Disclosure Act of 1998 into law. The media has dubbed it, the "The Good Samaritan" law. This was not even covered to any magnitude by the mainline media. This law will make it a lot easier for organizations to share information about their Y2K efforts without fear of being sued. This is an important law. The media, in my view should be getting this word out so that good old American 'lets help each other out' can kick in on a higher level. Heretofore, there has been a perception among companies at large that if they share their Y2K plans with another company, and if that information is faulty, they would be liable for lawsuit. That was a major deterrent to the flow of Y2K strategy information.

We need government to provide Y2K status on a regular basis. If we have to wait another full year for OMB's next report, it will be too late. Government status reports on Y2K readiness need to be more real-time. Y2K is an undertaking on the same scale, as the Persian Gulf War. The government needs to be reporting daily on Y2K, as it did for that war.

Are we asking ourselves 'What if?' scenarios at the macro level? Not obvious in any mainline media. The role of government in Y2K needs to be more proactive.

Y2K it is not a problem to be left up strictly to each individual organization. It is a much broader problem effecting all of society! And it requires government leadership and participation. If we do not get on it soon, our way of life will suffer to some extent, come year 2000. Top economists are saying that it could be, on the negative side, as bad as the recession of 1973. This is when we had all the problems from OPEC with importing oil. Prices for many other commodities when up. I remember having to wait in line with car to get gas. I remember the price of coffee and other staples subsequently going up in price.

However, before you go out and buy a wood burning stove for the living room, let me assure you that we will have heat, water and electricity. Also, there is no need to stock up on dehydrated food bundles or AK-47 ammunition. No need to convert your liquid assets to precious metals.

But from all practical considerations, we are going to have some problems to work through. Credit cards is one I would list right now. Too many issuers over too many networks of the good old plastic cards. I for one love to use my credit card and pay off my balance by end of next month's billing. I get a complete record at the end of the year. It is a beautiful thing! How many others do what I do? Many I know. So we may have to come up with some alternative ways come Y2K.

Although credit cards will be problematic, banks in general are doing quite well. Indeed, at this writing all banks are within 2%-3% of being fully compliant, even if the various networks around the country, which will transport their many credit card transactions, may not be. So there is no need to take out your savings and buy gold coins. But you may want to plan on alternatives to using your credit cards if you use them at all now. Remember that banks are insured through Federal Deposit Insurance Corporation (FDIC). FDIC has issued a mandate for all banks to be 100% Y2K ready by end of the first quarter of 1999. Non-compliant banks will face shutdown.

18

Y2K Fears and the Common Man

This final chapter in the book is more a commentary for people to consider as we approach the new millennium. It is my hope that we can try to keep the Y2K set of problems in perspective. Most people in my experience do not really want to take the time to understand the problem. Generally, they want an oversimplified explanation of the sort that can be contained in a sound bite or two on the evening news. And, this is exactly what the media is currently providing.

But if you have gotten this far in the book, you will have acquired a more comprehensive appreciation for the problem. Y2K is not going to be pretty. But we will get through it. It will take several years actually to be rid of it for good. After all, it took 30+ years to create.

With that, I would like to share with you my experience at a recent Y2K seminar held here in Pittsburgh.

I had the opportunity to attend a seminar sponsored by a local morning radio show regarding Year 2000 (Y2K). It was billed as a seminar that would define "everything" one needed to know about understanding and preparing for Y2K. They brought in a speaker who had been billed as having "National Marquee" appeal on the Y2K problem. There was a packed audience of several hundred people, mostly working folks, young families including children, and older couples. For 90 solid minutes the presenter talked and showed overhead slides which summarized numerous predictions regarding Y2K. For example: the banking system is going to collapse, our currency will become worthless, our food supply chains are going to crumble, planes will be falling from the sky, and this one I'm still chuckling about, "President Clinton is in reality the head of the Bible Belt Mafia, and is planning to use Y2K as the justification for becoming the Don of the entire civilized world". The speaker was not laughing throughout his presentation. He attempted to convey unequivocal doom and gloom.

Prior to the break, the speaker began a sales pitch to sell products right there, "at the tables to the right and left". The first product was a dehydrated food bundle for $5,000 that could support two people for one year. He suggested multiple bundles for larger families and groups, and did indeed give quantity purchase discounts. The food bundles were his solution to what he defined as the 'impending Y2K food shortage'. His other products available there included gold coins. He also had plans available to convert stocks, annuities and cash savings into gold coins. The gold coins, of course, were his solution to what he defines as the 'impending Y2K collapse of the currency and banking systems'.

During the break, some of us began to chat about the content of the seminar. A gentleman with his wife and another couple, all who appeared to be in there 30s and dressed casually, asked me what I thought about what the speaker was saying. I said it would not be appropriate for me to criticize at this time. The man asked " 'Why not?'-you bought your $15 ticket like the rest of us, and as far as I know we still have free speech"! I said, "O.K., everything he is saying is completely irrational, and all of his numbers are incorrect based on my research of the Y2K set of problems". He asked, "What do you think about his statement that we are going to run out of food?"

My reply was, "Lets look at McDonald's-you know home of the 'Big Mac'. A few years back they started working on getting their entire corporation Y2K compliant. Last year they achieved 100% compliance. Then they started, at their own expense, to reach out to their supplier chains. You know, where they get their hamburger patties, buns and so forth, from. (At this point a small crowd was gathering around us). Most of their suppliers are now Y2K compliant. By the end of this year (1998) 100% of their supplier chain is expected to be 100% compliant for Y2K. So, when the year 2000 comes you find that you can't get any food at the super market, keep in mind that you can always resort to going to your nearest McDonald's to get a quarter-pounder, Happy Meal, or whatever your pleasure may be." Everyone tuning in to our little sidebar laughed rather loud. It was like comic relief after a large dose of doom and gloom. At this point, if looks could kill, I would be dead about 7 times over because the entire staff of the presenter was staring me down, and apparently the expected crowd at the tables to the left and right never materialized.

Needless to say the remainder of the seminar was as severe as the first half. People trickled out for the balance of the evening. But the seminar brought home a very important point that we as a society need to face. Y2K is going to bring out many incredulous vendors of Y2K paraphernalia. It is certain that there will be many lecturers and vendors who will try to sell you Y2K products and services. For example: if the vendor tells you that we will have no heat or electricity, then that justifies his pitch for selling a portable generator or wood-burning stove. Many people impulse-buy based on fear, rather than on what they truly need.

Consequently, " caveat emptor", buyer beware, should be something that we as a society reemphasize anew in light of Y2K. Get the information you need to make an informed judgement about what you consider for purchase.

We will have some problems to work through with Y2K, but much work is being done across the country to make sure we will get through it. All of the banks will be ready, and in fact are already within 2%-3% of being fully compliant. I know that the speaker above refutes this. But I want you to know that the government, that insures your bank's deposits, has mandated that all banks must be 100% compliant by first quarter of 1999 or face shutdown.

Banks in many ways have been working on the problem for years. After all they make their money by loaning money. Long-term loans and mortgages, extending in term well beyond Y2K are among a bank's most lucrative products. To sell a loan that extends beyond 2000 they must be able to calculate principle, interest and balance on a daily basis for the life of the loan.

Similarly, all utilities have mandates from the government to be 100% compliant by June, 1999 or face loss of license to operate. We will have electricity, gas and water come Y2K.

Y2K will be resolved and become a non-issue. It is a man-made problem. Man is resolving it. It will require more work over the next few years to resolve completely. It will perhaps touch everyone in one way or another, from time to time, in the form of time loss and frustration. We've been there before. Who remembers when you couldn't 'fold, bend, or mutilate' your paycheck? Who remembers when you had to actually wait in line to deposit that paycheck? Remember having to pay for groceries in cash?

No one will starve or freeze to death solely because of Y2K. The message is clear to organizations across the country. If you want to do business in the Year 2000, you need to be Y2K compliant. The rest of the solution is good old Americana, can-do, spirit. Some call it 'capitalism'; others refer to it as 'free economy'. Some say it is basically supply and demand. Essentially, the desire to make money and continue to make money, and the desire to avoid losing money are perhaps the strongest motivators there are for organizations to get themselves Y2K compliant.

We consumers have more power than we realize over the Y2K set of problems. If, come Y2K, our usual supplier of goods is out of stock, we go to another supplier. Competition is another strong motivator. So if you are moved by Y2K fears to stock up on dehydrated food bundles and to liquidate your life savings into gold coins, keep in mind that it is highly unlikely that you will ever get back the value of the money you would have invested. But one thing is for sure, come Y2K. McDonald's will be closing in on 100 billion sold.

Epilogue

One fact which remains indisputable after over fifty years of computer technology turnover is that the digital computer today in its most fundamental form still must process everything at the binary, machine level in BITs. Many different computer technologies and methods have been developed to improve upon how we get BITs in and out of the computer to complete processing.

For instance, we have evolved from the vacuum tubes used on the early computers to today's microchips, semiconductors and super large scale- integrated circuitry. Nevertheless, after over 5 decades of evolution, the BIT remains an 'ON' or 'OFF' electrical state. And still today the Base 2 language of ones (1) and zero (0) is used by computer design programmers to represent these binary states respectively.

With the inception of networks, techniques were developed for coding the 'ON' or 'OFF' states from the computer into 'HIGH' or 'LOW' pulses for network transmission. And, as discussed in Chapter 14, many different types of networks have been and continue to be developed since the early days of the computer.

Given this, we can infer that digital computers and networks are intrinsically binary. As such machine level computer programmers can represent in binary language an infinite number of applications for the computer, using many different types and levels of coding that build on the requisite binary language. And when the computer translates these binary coded application programs they get processed electronically at nearly the speed of light. We as consumers see these programs in the form of application software packages, which are very, keyboard procedural, point and click, and do not require the user to know the binary language.

This is, principally, the major point of this book. Although developed over 50 years ago, the computer, and now the accompanying, multi-media computer network, still must process everything at the BIT & BYTE level. <u>And for the year 2000 and beyond, into the new millennium, information technology will continue to operate at the BIT and BYTE level. Binary language will continue to be the language of information technology into the new millennium.</u>

Common application software packages currently, include word-processing, spread-sheeting, databases and electronic mail. And we have even higher level language processors which request human input and provide output in natural language. There are great numbers of other application software examples. Too many to fit into this book. All shapes and sizes. With new ones coming out every day.

One common thread weaving through all of these applications is that no matter what level of coding is used, it all comes down to binary on the digital computer, to be processed inside the computer. That means 'ON' or 'OFF' electrical states on the computer and 'HIGH' or 'LOW' pulses over the network. Even though we users have been spared the need to know binary, the computer at the machine levels (i.e. inside where everything is electronic) still processes in binary. The network transmits in binary. It all comes down to the 'BIT'.

The size of the computer's main Data BUS is measured in BITs or BIT-width. Network transmission rates are based on number of BITs-per-second (bps). The BIT is critical to assessment of the computer's power in terms of size and speed. And, fundamental to measuring the speed of any network.

Unlike the BIT, the BYTE has been in evolution since the inception of the fully digital computer back in the 1940s. The BYTE has evolved from what it was on the first computer, in which the BYTE was used, only in its pure Base 2 form for mathematical calculations, to supporting today's multifaceted systems running various kinds of other textual, graphical, audio and other application software.

BYTEs are still made up of BITs. And the number of BITs per BYTE continues to be a variable for mathematical information. However for nonmathematical information the standardized character coding system being used on the computer predetermines the number of BITs per BYTE.

It is the character coding system that has been changing so much over the years. Today the UNICODE character coding system is considered to be state-of-the-art. A UNICODE character BYTE is 16 BITs long. In contrast, mathematical BYTEs are variable in length depending on how big of a number needs to be expressed in the Base 2 numbering system.

Consequently, knowing the BYTE is an important element in managing your computer resources. The BYTE enables us to "containerize" the coded BITs into well-defined units. If all we ever derived from the computer or the network was streams of BITs, there would be no meaningful information whatsoever beyond the mathematical, because, the computer's inherent language is Base 2, binary. At best we could only apply zeroes and ones to the many streams of BITs.

Memory and secondary storage are measured in BYTEs. The distinction between memory and storage is important because our method for measuring both is common. But the fact of the matter is that a memory BYTE is quite different from storage BYTE.

In memory, the BYTE is stored in a temporary, active cell. Such as in a microchip or semi-conductor, which holds millions of BYTE, size cells. The more memory chips installed on your computer the more you can process in active memory. However, when the power is turned off these chips are zeroed out. So it is vitally important that information BYTEs of any value are saved in permanent storage. This enables the information BYTEs to be retrieved at a subsequent computer session.

Secondary storage generally means permanent storage. This refers to your hard disk, diskette and other electro-magneto and electro-optical storage technologies. For example: CD-ROM, writable CDs and magnetic tape. Storage is considered permanent because once you have your files of BYTEs saved on some form of secondary storage, these files of BYTEs are safe for later retrieval and use.

One recurring question in many of the computer classes I have taught is "What do I do if the power goes off while I am working on the computer? Will my information be lost?" The answer is no, if you have saved your information on permanent storage. When power is restored and you restart your computer, you can retrieve the files of BYTEs, if you made it a point to do a save anytime prior to the power outage.

Therefore, knowing the BYTE is critical to fully comprehending the memory and storage used in computers and their corresponding networks. And, in truly understanding the Y2K set of problems. Y2K is a BYTE problem, whether it is embedded chip, general hardware or software related.

What I have summarized here constitutes the two major points of the book, namely, the BIT and the BYTE. Failure to know the BIT and the BYTE is not an option. The entire book is built upon these two very much abused and taken-for-granted computer network elements. Knowing the BIT and BYTE, I believe are fundamental requirements to computer network literacy, computer use and operations, as well as management at the operational, tactical and executive levels of any organization.

Finally, comprehension of the Year 2000 (Y2K) set of problems requires an understanding of the BIT and the BYTE. Y2K is fundamentally a BIT & BYTE problem. It could be renamed "The BIT & BYTE Problem of the 21st century".

From a BYTE perspective, computer and computer network hardware will need to be replaced by hardware manufactured to support the storage of a 4-BYTE calendar year field versus a 2-BYTE field. Also from a BYTE perspective, software application programs which process the calendar year using a 2-BYTE calendar year field will need to be modified to process the calendar year as a 4-BYTE field, and if a program cannot be modified it will need to be replaced. Non-compliant embedded chips will need to be located and replaced as soon as possible.

Y2K is a problem of serious magnitude effecting ultimately all layers of the economy and society. This is because all organizations today are completely dependent on computers and computer networks. Other developed countries will also have similar problems.

Understanding the nature and character of the Y2K set of problems means knowing the BIT and the BYTE. When Y2K comes with its ensuing chaos, you will at least comprehend its potential enormity. Perhaps you will be better able to manage your resources and contribute to the resolution of related problems at your place of work as well as in your home. Oh Yes! You can bet there will be problems. Y2K is not a problem affecting only one computer or a single network. But, all computers, all networks, located everywhere.

Index

About the author

Timothy V. Kelly has over 18 years of experience in the Information Technology field. His experience cuts across most

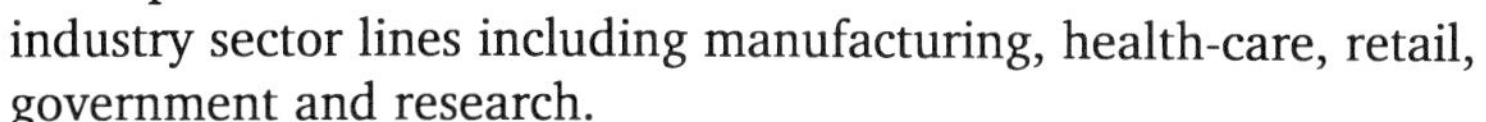

industry sector lines including manufacturing, health-care, retail, government and research.

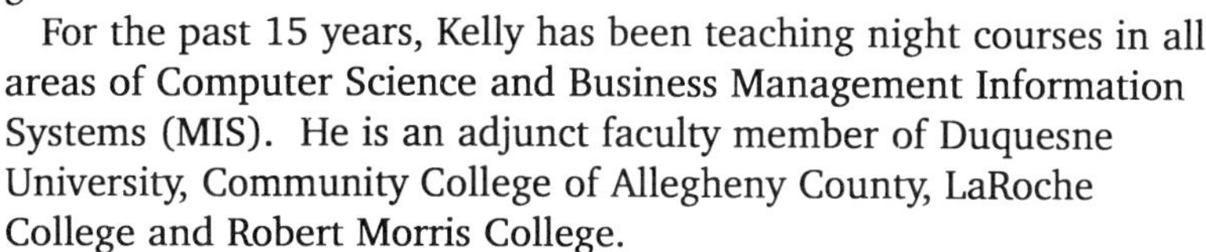

For the past 15 years, Kelly has been teaching night courses in all areas of Computer Science and Business Management Information Systems (MIS). He is an adjunct faculty member of Duquesne University, Community College of Allegheny County, LaRoche College and Robert Morris College.

Kelly holds undergraduate degrees in Mathematics and Sociology, Master of Arts from Duquesne University (1980), Master of Science in Information Science (1983) and has a post-graduate certificate in Telecommunications (1990) both at the University of Pittsburgh. He is a Magna Cum Laude graduate of Duquesne University.

In December 1990, Kelly was activated in the Navy by President Bush to complete work on a network interface needed to connect ships in the Persian Gulf via satellite with the computer network located at the Naval Station in Norfolk, Virginia.

In 1992, Kelly began consulting on a part-time basis. Under the company name of Network Technology Services (NTS), he has completed many engagements for Fortune 1000 companies and other organizations located in the Pittsburgh region.

More information is available on NTS on the WEB at http://members.aol.com/ntsy2k/y2k.html.

Over the years, Kelly has presented several Computer Network Literacy related seminars for many Pittsburgh Community-based organizations, including the Carnegie Library of Pittsburgh, the YMCA, and many social and church related organizations.

Kelly is the father of four children.